The Charlie Osburn Story

"You Gotta Give It All to Jesus"

The Charlie Osburn Story

"You Gotta Give It All to Jesus"

By Charlie Osburn
with
Fred Lilly

Good News Ministries
Box 77
Pensacola, FL 32591 USA

Good News of Divine Mercy
P.O. Box 1831
Belize City, Belize, Central America

Reprinted 2000
Harvey Whitney Books Company
4906 Cooper Rd., P.O. Box 42696
Cincinnati, Ohio 45242 USA
www.hwbooks.com

Cover photo and design by Michael Andaloro.

Printed in the United States of America.

Library of Congress Control Number: 00-132411

International Standard Book Number: 0-929375-24-6 (previous ISBN 0-89283-287-8)

Contents

ONE

The Downhill Slide

"YOU GOTTA GIVE IT ALL TO JESUS."

My family was not particularly religious. I suppose my parents believed in God—I remember his name coming up in conversation once in a while. But, except for occasional weddings and funerals, we never went to church.

When a Catholic priest named James Smith first spoke those words to me, I had no idea what he meant. Give *what* to Jesus? How? It was all pious talk. But as Father Smith continued to tell me the truth about God, how he loved me and wanted me to have a better life, I saw that Father Smith was much more sane than I was.

I finally swallowed my pride and invited Jesus Christ into my life. I began to change, to grow, to prosper. God poured his love into my heart, healed my broken family and my sick body, and gave me a ministry. That ministry, serving my God and my church as a Catholic lay evangelist, is more rewarding and exciting than I ever imagined life could be.

I would like to tell you how this happened. Before God could bless me in this way, I had to learn some very important lessons about life. I learned them the hard way.

We all come into the world the same way, created by God and born of human parents. God creates us for a purpose—to know him, to love him, and to serve him. But none of this was communicated to me as a boy growing up in a small town in

North Carolina. At a very early age, the things of the world began to excite me. Material possessions brought me what I thought was happiness. Money in the pocket, spending money, selling things for profit—these were the things that brought me joy and fulfillment. Making money became my definition of the purpose of life; money itself became my god. So I decided that I would find ways to make as much money as possible.

I quickly learned that I had the knack for making money. One of my earliest successes was selling lemonade during the Second World War. Sugar was rationed then but my family received a greater ration of sugar than most because my father was in the service. I made lemonade with real sugar in a big wooden washtub and pulled it on a wagon down to the tobacco market. People loved that ice-cold lemonade sweetened with sugar on hot days. I made a big profit and it excited me a great deal. My pockets were loaded, so I was happy.

As I grew older and more successful, I began to think about God. I decided that God liked successful people. My spiritual philosophy was "God helps those who help themselves," and I found it quite easy to help myself. Not only was it easy for me to make money, but people admired me for it. Some were even jealous. Thrusting my chest out like a proud peacock, I'd show off my new car and bulging wallet. When I noticed that people were admiring or envious, I showed off even more openly. I wanted people to notice Charlie Osburn.

After graduating from high school, I spent ten years in the military, pulling extra duty and cutting hair to fatten my paycheck.

I met my wife when I was transferred to Pensacola, Florida. She was the first person I met when I arrived at the Naval Station to present my transfer orders. After she finished processing my papers, I asked her to direct me to a restaurant where I could get a good hamburger.

When I arrived at the restaurant Jeanne was there with

some of her friends. They asked me to sit with them, and I was attracted to Jeanne from that moment on. We dated and finally decided to get married. Because I loved Jeanne so much, I wanted to understand and appreciate every aspect of her life, but I just couldn't understand why she was so committed to the Catholic Church. Religion had never meant anything to me. But as we discussed our future life together she told me that she would continue to be active in her church. She also insisted that we raise our children in the Catholic faith.

Because of Jeanne's adamance, I decided to investigate the Catholic Church and began talking with the principal of Pensacola Catholic High, Msgr. William Houck (now the Catholic bishop of Jackson, Mississippi). Msgr. Houck taught me a great deal about the church and displayed the same intense devotion to it as my wife-to-be. So for the first time in my life I began to think seriously about committing my life to God and to a church.

Later I was transferred to a naval base in Sanford, Florida, and was separated from Jeanne, which gave me more time to think about our future. I decided to take instructions at the local Catholic parish, and at the end of the course, only a few weeks before our wedding, the priest baptized me in a private ceremony.

"I've got a surprise for you," I told Jeanne when I returned to Pensacola a few days before our wedding. "I am now a baptized Catholic."

Jeanne was thrilled. She picked up the phone and called the priest who was to perform the wedding ceremony, and arranged for a nuptial mass. (In 1956 the church did not permit masses during a marriage ceremony unless both partners were Catholic.) Our wedding day was truly glorious.

A few years later I was discharged from the navy and I put all the money I had into opening a canvas shop. Seven years later I sold the shop and leased a restaurant, carefully saving and planning for the day when I could open my own. Four years later I built a restaurant and office complex in Pensacola, Florida.

I was very proud of those achievements. In only eleven years I had worked my way up from a poor boy to being proprietor of one of the most expensive restaurants in our affluent city. The rich and the successful all dined at my restaurant. I was, I thought, making quite a mark on the world. At a frenzied pace I developed my business, purchased everything I could possibly want, and established my family as the envy of our community.

Nor was my success limited to the business field. I got into politics. I was appointed the first honorary mayor of the township of Warrington, Florida, and I lost a race for county commissioner by only a few votes. I schemed, I manipulated, I took advantage of people, all for my own gain.

But the pressure in my life was intense. At thirty-five I began to drink "just a little to settle my nerves." The demands of business, politics, social life, and family responsibilities added up to eighteen-hour days, seven days a week. I thought I needed a little nip now and then. I told myself I deserved it.

But the more responsibilities I took on, the more my family life grew strained, and the more heavily I began to drink to relieve the pressure. I was an alcoholic, but I denied it. I blamed my problems on everyone else—my wife, my children, the IRS—but never on myself.

One morning I woke up disillusioned with the whole world. Here I was, a millionaire, successful in the eyes of everyone who knew me. But I was an empty, broken man, and I knew it. And I was angry—angry with my wife and my children, angry with myself. I was angry with everyone and everything in the whole world. Nothing could satisfy me. The harder I worked and the more money I made, the more money I wanted.

It was the same with my drinking. The more I drank, the more it took to satisfy me. It was even true of my smoking—first a pack a day, then two packs, then three packs.

Caught in this vicious cycle, I found myself at forty-three with high blood pressure, a hiatal hernia, and a number of nervous conditions for which I took several medications to keep me from shaking.

I was a broken, miserable man. It took more than fifteen years for me to realize that my choices in life had led me to this. When I discovered what I had become, I was desperate. I knew something had to change, but even at that point I never dreamed that the very money and success I craved caused most of my problems. I looked for someone to blame, and I found the perfect scapegoat in my wife, Jeanne.

"She's the problem. In twenty years, she hasn't done a thing for me except spend my money and give me a hard time."

Our relationship had deteriorated to the point where we had absolutely nothing to talk about. I'd leave the house in the morning and come home at night without ever saying a word to her. If I was leaving town for two or three days, I wouldn't tell her. I would just come home, change my clothes, reload my pockets with money, and leave without so much as a nod in her direction.

So I began to plan how to leave her. I had to proceed slowly. I was the mayor, after all, and I couldn't let a scandal harm my chances for continued success and prestige.

In the midst of this, I renewed my acquaintance with Father James Smith, a priest I had first met when I joined the Catholic Church at the age of twenty-three. We had been friends for a number of years until he was assigned to a parish in another place. He was gone for fourteen years. Then one day he returned to Pensacola and came to the restaurant to see me.

I was really excited to see him and told him so.

"Well, praise the Lord, Charles. It's exciting to see you, too" was his reply. I ignored the "praise the Lord" and asked him how he'd been.

"Wonderful," he said.

That startled me. When I asked that question, most people told me how terrible their lives were, playing what I call the "ain't it awful" game: "Oh, it's just awful, Charlie. Don't know if I'm going to make it. I've got problems at home; problems with my business; problems down at city hall. Ain't it awful?"

So that's what I did with Father Smith—for about two hours. I went on and on about what a terrible state my life was in. After my monologue he looked me in the eye and said, "Charlie, I've got good news for you."

"He wants to lend me some money" was my first thought. I was convinced that priests carried a good amount of cash around with them. Since I had just finished telling Father Smith that I had lost a great deal of money gambling on golf games, I thought he would advance me a few thousand to tide me over during my dry spell.

But he didn't. He simply invited me to his house. "I've got some exciting things to tell you about the church," he said.

I was a good Catholic in those days—by my own definition. I went to Mass every Sunday regardless of what I had done during the week. For several years I had even gone to Mass every day. My fervor had lapsed quite a bit during the previous few years as my life fell apart. I kept going to church on Sunday only because it would be bad for business if people noticed I stopped. For a mayor concerned with social standing and future political ambitions, it was important to be seen in church, especially if you've got a restaurant only three blocks away.

When Father Smith told me that the church had more to offer me, I didn't know what to think. I'd done everything I thought there was to do: I'd been a Knight of Columbus, president of the Holy Name Society. I belonged to the Legion of Mary, the Society of St. Vincent de Paul, and I helped take up the collection every Sunday.

"Why in the world," I asked myself, "would he tell me

there is anything more in this church? I've tried everything it has."

I later discovered that the problem had not been with the church, but with me. I was more concerned about "achieving success" in the church than I was about having a personal relationship with the head of the church, Jesus Christ. And all my service in the church I had done for Charlie Osburn, rather than for Jesus. Yet all my activities would not fill the void within me. I needed the Lord.

I don't know why I accepted Father Smith's invitation to hear more about what the church had to offer. But I did. The next day I was knocking on the rectory door. I'll never forget that meeting. I wasn't ten feet inside when he pointed his finger at me and said, "Charlie, you've got to give it all to Jesus."

"What?" I thought. "Jesus doesn't want any of the problems I have. I'm a mess."

But I said only, "Yes, Father," because, like any good Catholic, I knew that no matter what a priest said to me, I should always be diplomatic. I didn't tell him that I didn't have the slightest idea what he was talking about. I went over to the couch and sat down, and he began to tell me things that I thought were really strange.

"Charlie," he said, "do you know that Jesus loves you?"

"There's no way he can love me. I've done too many terrible things," I replied.

"Oh yes, he does," Father said.

"Father Smith," I said. "You know me and God knows me. But he knows me a lot differently than you know me. And there is no way he can love me because he knows the kind of person I am and the kinds of things I have done."

"Charlie," he answered. "I don't care what you've done. I don't care how bad you think you are. Jesus loves you in spite of yourself. Jesus loves you totally, completely, and unconditionally."

I'd never heard a priest talk like this before. I asked, "Are you sure?"

"I'm sure," he said. "If you had been the only person living on this earth, Jesus would have come and died just for you."

"Me?" I thought. "Old, no good, lying and cheating me?"

We talked for four hours. I listened to things that I had never heard before. At the end Father Smith invited me to come back the following week.

"You know, I think I will," I answered.

I returned to my restaurant, sat down on a barstool in the lounge, got a scotch and water, and thought about what Father Smith had said. I thought about it for the entire week. But by the time Monday came around I didn't really want to go back. Couldn't I just say I was too busy? But something in me said, "Why don't you just go back one more time."

Monday afternoon found me knocking again on the rectory door, and as soon as I walked inside it was, "Charlie, you've got to give it all to Jesus."

"How can I give Jesus anything?" I thought. To my mind, Jesus was the big "eye in the sky," carefully noting everything I did right and everything I did wrong. I had so many more wrongs than rights that God was punishing me. He was beating me to death, and I didn't know how to get him off of me.

I just couldn't accept this love concept of Father Smith's. It was too much. I knew this priest was a nice guy, and I was grateful to him for wanting to tell me nice things, but I just couldn't believe that Jesus would love me.

I also knew that I was dying spiritually. I was desperate and full of despair, yet I could not believe the things that would save my life. I was a drowning man refusing to grab a life preserver because I was sure it wouldn't hold my weight.

Father Smith was way ahead of me. He sat me down and began to tell me things which I realized years later were some of the most important things I was to hear in my entire life.

"Charlie," he said, "do you remember when Pope Pius XII died in 1958?" Actually I didn't. I remembered that every few years a pope would die, and we'd get a new pope, and then he'd die, and we'd get another new one. None of it meant much to me.

"Well," he said, "let me tell you what happened. After he died, the college of cardinals came together to select a new pope. They deliberated and prayed for many days, but they just could not agree on who should be the new pope. Ballot after ballot came and went, and still no agreement. Finally, they decided to elect an old cardinal from Venice who would be the caretaker of the Vatican for a few years. After he died, the cardinals would try again to elect someone who would be pleasing to the world. This man, Cardinal Roncalli, became Pope John XXIII."

Pope John, Father Smith told me, was a man who prayed a great deal and earnestly listened to the Holy Spirit, and his prayer produced in him the conviction that the Catholic Church needed fresh air. So, much to the surprise and chagrin of many of the cardinals who elected him pope, he called a council of the world's bishops to be held in Rome. And that council, the pope said, was to renew the fervor of the day of Pentecost in the church in our day.

"What does that have to do with me?" I thought. I didn't say this, of course, but I thought it the whole time Father Smith talked excitedly about the pope and the council and the signs and wonders that followed it.

I had just begun to wonder if he had forgotten who he was talking to when he said, "Charlie, you are the church."

"What?" I said right back. "The church is that big building down on Fifth and Main with the stained-glass windows and the beautiful crosses."

"No, you are the church," he insisted. "The church is the people who use that big building to worship God. The church is all the individual men and women who come together to hear God's voice and receive his blessings."

I had never heard that before. Me, a living, breathing church? Me, with all my faults and all my problems, a temple of the Holy Spirit and a brother to Jesus Christ?

Father Smith then began to talk about the outpouring of the Holy Spirit that Catholics had been experiencing ever since that council. Then he stopped and invited me to come back in a week.

I had planned on this being the last of our little chats. But this talk about Pentecost and the Holy Spirit and ordinary people like me being the church intrigued me, and I wanted to find out more. He had told me only part of the story and I was hooked. I had to come back the next week to find out what happened.

A week later I returned, and the scene at the door was repeated once again. "Charlie," Father Smith said, "you've got to give it all to Jesus."

I still couldn't see how anyone could give anything to Jesus, but I held my tongue and said only, "Yes, Father."

After I sat down he looked at me and said, "Charlie, Jesus wants to heal your body."

"Oh no," I thought. "Is he a faith healer? Everyone knows that faith healers are phonies. God just doesn't do things like that. That's what doctors are for."

"Jesus wants to deliver you from alcohol," he said.

"Well, I'm not sure I want to be delivered," I thought.

"Jesus wants to heal your relationship with your wife."

"Now wait," I said. "I know that God is great and good, but even he can't heal that. My marriage is beyond healing. It's finished, and I'm not sure I would even want it healed."

"Jesus wants to introduce you to his love," he replied.

I was really puzzled. I couldn't understand. I didn't know what love was. I had never really loved anyone, and I didn't know how to love. I knew how to take advantage of people. I knew how to make money. I could wheel and deal just about anybody out of just about anything. But I couldn't love anyone, not even my wife.

So I just thought, "Dear God, this poor priest is going down the tubes."

I don't know if Father Smith knew how I was reacting, but he went on telling me that God had created everyone out of his great love, and that I could turn to him for forgiveness and healing and live a new kind of life.

I didn't believe this. I didn't believe that God had created everyone to receive his blessings equally. I believed that he had created me a bit better than most people. After all, I had more money and more energy than most. And he was punishing me more than other people because I had done more bad things.

It was sad that I thought this. I had gone to church every Sunday for more than fifteen years. I had heard hundreds of hours of sermons. But still I did not understand. All my life I had been greedy, selfish, arrogant, and had justified it all to myself. I had demanded success from myself without ever considering the needs and desires of anyone else. I gave no thought to my wife or my children. I was a hard man, and now this priest was telling me that God could melt that hardness and give me something I couldn't earn or buy or find in any other way. God could give me love, he said, and enable me to love other people. In that love I could find real happiness.

Father Smith invited me back the following Monday. Once again, in my thoughts, I resisted. The meetings interfered with my golf game. But something was happening inside of me. I was in a turmoil, drinking more heavily than ever. So I agreed to come.

The next week I returned and knocked on the door. When I came in Father Smith was standing in the kitchen with his back to me stirring a cup of coffee. He wheeled around and, as loud and hard as he could, he shouted, "Charlie, you've got to give it all to Jesus."

"Well," I shouted back, "you tell me what to give him, and I'll give it to him."

"You've got to give him your wife."
"Man, he can have her."
"You've got to give him your kids."
"They're his," I said.
"Charlie, Jesus wants to be Lord of your life."
"You tell me how to let Jesus be the Lord of my life and I'll do it."

Father Smith told me to kneel down on the floor and I did. He put his hand on my head and said a prayer that began something like this:

"Father, you promised to send the Holy Spirit to anyone who would ask."

He looked at me and said, "Charlie, do you desire the Holy Spirit of God?"

"I do," I said.

"Father," he continued, "Charlie desires to make Jesus Christ the Lord of his life, don't you, Charlie?"

"Yes," I said.

And he said, "Father, by faith we receive your gift and we thank you."

Then he asked me something that I wished he hadn't asked: "How do you feel?"

"I don't feel anything," I said.

Father Smith had described the Holy Spirit to me as someone who comes like a bolt of lightning. I was expecting something extraordinary and wonderful. As far as I could tell, nothing had happened.

In my disappointment I thought I heard a voice say, "You dirty, rotten, no good lying bum, you'll never get it."

Then I heard another voice say, "God will never refuse anyone who seeks after the Holy Spirit."

At that time I knew nothing about spiritual warfare and the influence that Satan tries to exert on believers. But I knew which voice I wanted to believe.

I got up off the floor to go home. As I walked out the door Father Smith said, "Charlie, we've got a prayer meeting at the church on Wednesday nights. Would you like to come?"

"What kind of meeting?" I asked.

"A prayer meeting."

It sounded very un-Catholic to me.

"Does the bishop know about this?" I asked.

"Yes," he answered. "The bishop knows all about our prayer meeting. He asked me to start it."

If it had the approval of the bishop it must be all right, I thought. Still, the very idea of a prayer meeting in our church struck me as strange and something to avoid. I said I'd think about attending and then I left for home.

When I arrived home I called my wife and children to me and said, "I don't understand what Father Smith is telling me about the Holy Spirit. I don't understand this experience with Jesus Christ he keeps talking about. But if what he's telling me is true, I can't afford to miss it. Now, would any of you like to go to the prayer meeting with me to receive whatever it is we're supposed to receive?"

My wife agreed to go, but each of our five children refused. I knew they thought I was just on another crazy fling, working early for the next election to get the church vote.

So when Wednesday came my wife and I went to the prayer meeting. When I walked into the room and saw people with their hands raised in the air, I thought, "What in the world is this? I am really in the wrong place!" I wanted to leave, but my wife was already sitting down, so I did too.

When I sat down I sat on both of my hands because I wasn't about to raise them in the air. It seemed to me the silliest thing I had ever seen—all these people with their hands in the air and praying out loud.

This went on for two hours. I just kept looking at my watch thinking, "When does this thing end? I've got to get out of here."

TWO

Conversion

THAT PRAYER MEETING STRUCK ME as bizarre. However, even though I wanted to leave as fast as I could, I was intrigued by one strange sight. Every once in a while Father Smith would boom out a message in a language I didn't understand. I knew that he knew Latin, but I was surprised to hear him speak it so well.

Then another man I knew who had only a high school education like myself started speaking in Latin just like Father Smith. "Now how did he ever learn Latin?" I wondered.

I hadn't yet heard about the ancient gift of speaking in unknown tongues, and if I had, I would probably have fled the room. As it was, I was growing very concerned. "If the people of Warrington ever hear about me being with people like this, I'll be ruined," I thought.

I'd been very careful all my life of my public image. Now, I thought, everything I had worked so hard for was in serious jeopardy.

As the meeting was winding down one of the leaders asked if anyone needed prayer. This was my opportunity.

"Sure," I said, "you can all pray for me." Then I gave everyone a big smile, grabbed my wife's hand, and headed for the door. But before I got halfway across the room, a man put two chairs in front of us and said, "Have a seat."

"What for?" I asked.

"We're going to pray for you."

"Right here in front of everybody? You must be kidding."

"No, we're not kidding. We're going to pray for you right now."

I was trapped, so I sat down on one chair and my wife sat on the other. Then a number of people gathered around and put their hands on me. One woman knelt down in front and put her hand on my knee.

"This is nuts," I thought.

Then they all prayed loudly for about fifteen minutes in English and in what I thought was Latin. After they were done, the woman whose hand was still on my knee looked up and spoke to me.

"Charlie, how do you feel?"

"Terrible," I said. "I wish I weren't here. Right now I honestly think that there may not even be a God. I feel like an empty hole."

So they prayed again, louder than ever. I glanced over at my wife, who was grinning from ear to ear. When they finally finished, I grabbed Jeanne and left as fast as I could work my way through the room.

For the next two days I thought constantly about my experience at the prayer meeting. I finally figured out that the people at the meeting hadn't been speaking Latin at all. They had been speaking in tongues, and I wanted no part of it. I was angry and embarrassed to think I had just sat there while people I knew babbled away in a language they didn't understand.

Father Smith, however, was persistent. Later that week I went to another meeting at another Catholic church and found that these people did the same bizarre things. My distaste increased when I saw an elderly woman sitting in the back wholeheartedly praising Jesus. She was very poor, and I thought, "How can she do that when she's in rags?" It seemed incredible to me that she could talk about how good God was. I had no idea that her love for Jesus was greater than all the earthly treasure I had worked so hard to accumulate. She was speaking to Jesus from her heart.

Father Smith knew that I was disgusted, embarrassed, and afraid to meet this new wave of the Spirit in the church. But instead of leaving me alone, he kept up his offensive. He called me one day and said, "Charlie, the church tells us to be ecumenical."

"What's that?" I asked.

"We're supposed to have fellowship with our Protestant brothers and sisters. I want you to come to a Protestant meeting with me."

"It's a sin to go to a Protestant service," I said.

"No," he corrected me. "The bishops have told us very clearly to be open to Protestants."

"Father Smith," I said, "are you sure you're in good standing with the bishop?"

"I am."

"Well," I said, "which Protestant church do you want to go to?"

"The meeting is not at a church," he said. "It's over at the Holiday Inn."

A service at the Holiday Inn! I was stunned. Father Smith wanted me to go to a Protestant service at the same Holiday Inn where I went drinking with my friends. I didn't want to go, but I was too ashamed to say why.

Father Smith didn't give me long to think about it, though. "I'll pick you up in fifteen minutes," he said and hung up.

I went. I looked down at the floor as Father Smith and I passed the bar. I was sure my buddies were in there, laughing at me for going with a priest to this church service. As soon as I walked into the meeting room, I was the center of attention. Everyone knew me because I was a politician. I overheard comments like "That's Charlie Osburn. Can you believe it?" and "Won't it be great if we get him?" I was never so embarrassed in my life.

Then a woman with a puzzled look on her face approached me and asked, "Why are you here?"

"I've come to be baptized in the Holy Spirit," I said.

I still don't know why those words came out of my mouth. It wasn't what I intended to say. But God was working in me, and perhaps my body wanted to follow him even if my mind wasn't quite ready to go along.

I doubt if I'm the first person who walked into one of these meetings and asked to be baptized in the Holy Spirit. But my statement had an immediate effect. Before I knew it, I was surrounded by about 200 people. They started to pray, and one man boomed out in a loud voice, "In the name of Jesus I command you, Satan, to get out of here."

"*I* have to get out of here," I muttered to myself. "This is too much."

"I'm leaving," I said, and I tried to, but the circle of people was so tight I couldn't escape. I was trapped, trapped in the Holiday Inn in the middle of a circle of fanatics who were praying about Satan. It was bad enough not to understand what was going on around me, but I couldn't figure out what was happening *inside* me either.

I was so upset that I didn't talk to Father Smith all the way home. But I did think about the people I had seen at these meetings. I realized that they all seemed to be truly happy. Everybody walked around with big smiles, in contrast to my constant frown. Their joy made me realize how unhappy I was.

"These people," I thought, "have something important and I want it." When I got home I laid down on my bed and began to cry.

And I prayed.

"Lord Jesus, if there is really anything to all this talk about the Holy Spirit, would you please give it to me? Lord Jesus, if you are really a God who comes personally into people's lives, would you become the Lord of my life? Lord Jesus, if you truly heal people, would you please heal my body?"

I had reached the bottom. I was a sick man—sick in body and sick in heart. I wept for a long time and finally fell asleep.

When I woke up the next morning I couldn't figure out what was wrong with me. I didn't know whether to laugh or cry, to scream or to sing. I began to think that I was cracking up. But I felt good, so good that I didn't care. For the first time in years, I had awakened without a headache, and there was no sign of the hiatal hernia that had bothered me for ten years. I felt like a new man, physically and spiritually cleansed and reborn.

The first problem of the day came quickly. It was my turn to go to the hospital and help my wife's grandmother eat her lunch. We had never been able to get along. Sparks flew whenever we were in the same room. That morning, however, I saw a different person when I walked into the hospital room. It wasn't the same woman I had quarreled with for twenty years.

"Hello, Momsy, it's so good to see you." And I meant it.

"Get away from me," she barked.

Despite her rebuff, which had come from many years of mutual disdain, I knew my heart had changed. I just wanted to hug her, but I knew this wasn't the time to try it.

After finishing at the hospital I jumped in my car to return to the restaurant. Driving down Navy Boulevard, just three blocks from my restaurant, I passed an old Bible book store. Suddenly, I knew that Jesus was the Lord of my life. I knew that the God of heaven had answered the prayers of a broken man. It was as if a light had suddenly flicked on in my head: I experienced the presence of the Lord Jesus Christ in my life.

As I realized this, Jesus flooded my soul with his love. He came into my car and into my body and loved me in a way I'd never experienced love before.

I eased the car over to the side of the road, lay down on the seat, and raised my hands toward heaven. Raising my hands, which I had disdained when I saw other people do it, no longer seemed strange. It was a natural act of submission to God and praise of the one who had forgiven my sins, healed my body, and filled my soul with a love that is impossible to describe yet impossible to forget.

I was completely overcome with gratitude. I thanked God in every way imaginable, and, when my vocabulary was exhausted, I began to pray in a wonderful, strange tongue as I had heard so many other people pray. I didn't try to—it just flowed from my heart. I was praising God in his own language, worshipping him in the Spirit.

I have no idea how long I lay there praising God in tongues. I know I wanted to stay there forever. I felt the way Peter must have felt on the Mount of Transfiguration when he said, "Lord, let us put up a tent." I felt like I'd gone to heaven, and I didn't want it to end. The anger, the hatred, the depression, the anxiety I had been carrying in my heart for years left in an instant. I felt them go. The cloud of hurt from all of the years of ambition and frustration evaporated, and a joy I'd never experienced took its place.

Finally, I sat up. I was so happy I just had to tell somebody what had happened to me. I started the engine, pulled the car around into the parking lot of the Gospel Lighthouse Bible book store, ran inside, and said, "I've got to tell someone what just happened to me."

A woman named Rose Rhymes ran out of the stock room, looked at me, and beamed.

"Charlie Osburn," she said, "praise God. I'm glad to see you finally accepted Jesus into your life. I've been praying for you for three years, Charlie."

All I could do was shout, "Hallelujah! Glory to God!"

I've been shouting ever since. People are sometimes offended by my shouting, but I can't help it. Jesus reached into the very depths of hell and retrieved me, a terrible sinner. I'll shout praises to him as long as there is breath in my lungs. In fact, I believe we'll all be shouting praises in heaven. We're just in training for it here on earth!

I left that store feeling like I was walking on air, a feeling which stayed with me all day. And God had another surprise in store for me. He healed my marriage.

The very moment I saw my wife, I saw her with spiritual eyes. "Dear God, what a wonderful woman you gave me," I thought. I had never been able to see her spiritual beauty before. In all our years of marriage, I had looked at her only from a worldly point of view. And she usually fell short of what I thought I needed. But now I began to see her as God wanted me to see her.

What did I see? An original masterpiece fashioned by God's own hands. An absolute gem, revealing in an earthly way some of God's perfection, a measure of his divine life. I fell in love with Jeanne that day, and we've had a wonderful relationship ever since. We stopped building our relationship on the things of the world and built it in Jesus instead. Of course it took time to learn how to relate to one another in a new way. You don't change the bad habits of a lifetime in a few minutes. I had abused Jeanne for years, and I had to learn to treat her properly. Jeanne had to learn how to love me and how to encourage me.

Changing our behavior wasn't easy for either of us, but God was with us during those months of struggle and growth. With his help we learned how to love each other and lay down our lives for each other the way the gospel teaches.

During the days following my encounter with Jesus Christ, the Lord stripped the scales from my eyes. He let me see what the riches I had craved really were: illusions and disappointments. Everything that I had strived so hard to obtain lost its appeal to me. All I wanted to do was to love my wife and my children and to begin working for the Lord.

I am not saying that everyone who has accumulated worldly wealth mishandles it the way I did. I treated money and possessions the same way I treated alcohol: I abused them. The only way I could respond was to renounce the things I couldn't control, and I am certain that this was God's desire for me.

However, I have known fine Christian people who are wealthy in the world's eyes. They have learned how to handle their wealth in a righteous way. Some of them have even become supporters of my evangelistic ministry and other ministries which build up the body of Christ.

As my life with God developed I would lie awake at night and beg him to allow me to work for him. "Lord Jesus, please let me be a witness for you. Lord, give me a ministry so I can tell people about you."

It wasn't long before the Lord answered that prayer. I began to witness about Jesus to every person who came in the door of my restaurant. Some people responded positively, but not everyone liked the new Charlie Osburn. One night when I was back in the kitchen singing at the top of my lungs, my wife came to the door and said, "We just lost four more customers." That happened regularly.

"Glory to God" was all I could reply. I knew who Jesus was and what he had done for me, and I couldn't keep still. I intended to tell the world about him, no matter what it cost me.

Not long afterward I purchased time on a local radio station to share what I had learned about the love of Jesus. One day a couple walked in the front door of the restaurant with the biggest painting of Jesus I had ever seen.

"We've been listening to your radio program," they said. "The Lord told us to give this to you."

I hung the painting in the foyer of the restaurant, and under it I put a sign that read "the boss."

Not all my customers were pleased with that either. My restaurant was a first-class coat-and-tie kind of place. We catered to the rich, and the rich did not think highly of the things I was doing. That was all right with me. For years I had tried to please and imitate the wealthy, and all it brought me was misery. It was a dead-end road. Now all I wanted was to follow Jesus and witness for him. I wanted to think like Jesus. I wanted to act like Jesus. I wanted to do the kinds of things that Jesus did.

I read the Bible every chance I had. I would read the New Testament and marvel at what Jesus did. He was the only Son of the almighty God, who came to earth in obedience to his Father, emptied himself of all that he was, took on the form of a slave, and died because he loved me—Charlie Osburn. When I understood what Jesus had done for me, I began studying his life.

One thing about Jesus particularly impressed me: he never sold anything. He only gave things away. As I thought about that I began to pray, "Lord, I want to be like you."

God began to answer this prayer by teaching me about trust. Once I woke up in the middle of the night and sensed that the Lord was speaking to me.

"Do you trust me, Charlie?" the Lord asked.

"I trust you with my life," I said.

The next night I woke up with this same internal voice saying, "Charlie, do you really trust me?"

"Lord, I do," I said.

He asked me the same question every night for a week. Finally I said, "Lord, if I'm not trusting you, please show me where."

"I thought you gave me everything," I heard the Lord say.

"But I did," I replied.

"You haven't given your restaurant over to me."

"Of course I have, Lord. I even put your picture up right there in front where everyone can see it."

Then the Lord told me that he wanted me to radically change the way I did business at my restaurant. He wanted me to give the food away rather than sell it. He wanted me to imitate Jesus who had never sold anything, but had given away everything he had, even his very life.

I was dumbfounded.

"I can't run a restaurant that way, Lord."

I balked at the very idea. It was easy to *say* I trusted God. But give away the food in my restaurant? It would destroy the business! I started screaming like a stuck pig. But God didn't give up on me. He was asking me to deny myself, pick up my cross, and follow him. The waking up in the middle of the night began all over again.

"Charlie, do you trust me? Do you really trust me?"

This time I was honest.

"No, Lord, I guess I don't. Please teach me how to trust you."

"I want to be Lord of everything: your body and soul, your wife, your children, even your restaurant."

"How will I make a living? How will I feed my family? How will I pay for the education of my children?"

"Do you trust me, Charlie?"

My answer was different now. "I don't know if I trust you, Lord, but I really want to."

God wanted to strip away the thing that had been my god all my life—money. It hurt like the dickens.

A few nights after I realized this, I was working in the kitchen at the restaurant and praying in tongues. I suddenly had a vision of all of God's creation. I saw the depth, the beauty, and the greatness of the Lord's universe in a way I had never perceived it before.

Then the Lord spoke to me and said, "Charlie, I did all of this for you."

I jumped for joy over that revelation. Literally. Right there in the kitchen. Then God said, "Everything I've done from the beginning of time I did with you in mind."

"Lord," I said, "you're too good."

I began to praise and worship God for all that he had done. Then the Lord asked, "Charlie, if I've done all of this, don't you think I can run a little restaurant like this?"

The next day I took my menu to a printer and asked him to print it again, without the prices.

"What for?" he asked. "Are you going to change the prices every day?"

"No," I said. "God's telling me to give my food away."

"What?" he said. "Charlie, you're crazy. You can't do this."

I had a tough time with the printer. He didn't want to do it because he thought I was losing my mind, and I thought he might be right. Losing money was not my idea of fun. Yet God had told me that he would take care of me.

The printer persisted. "Charlie, you just can't do this."

"I have no choice," I answered. "Jesus Christ has become Lord of my life. I have surrendered everything to him. I know people will think I'm a fool, but I'd rather be a fool for Jesus than successful in this world."

In the end he gave in and printed the menu without prices. I felt as though I were hanging over the edge of a precipice the day I put those new menus into my customers' hands. I knew that Jesus was in charge. I also knew that the people coming in to dine could take advantage of me. I had never in all my life been in that position.

My new policy quickly drove away the last of my rich customers, and the restaurant began to fill up with the poor. The word got around that there was a crazy man down on Navy Boulevard giving away his food. My new patrons were alcoholics, prostitutes, and street people of all kinds. These were the poor whom society had rejected, the ones the world had no place for. Now they had a place where they could break bread.

At first I was thrilled with this development. God was using my restaurant to reach society's outcasts. However, when the thrill wore off, my old fears returned.

"God, what are you doing?" I asked one night when a scantily clad girl came in. She was wearing short-shorts, a T-shirt, and nothing else. She came in drunk with six other people and sat down at a table in the middle of the restaurant. They ate so much I wondered where on earth they were putting it.

I knew they weren't going to give me a cent even though they were eating a mountain of food. We had cut a hole in the counter where the cash register had been and posted a sign welcoming donations for the ministry. After three months, we hadn't received any money at all. We were rapidly running out of money and out of food in the pantry. I began to panic.

"What are you doing, Lord?" I prayed.

THREE

Restaurant Evangelist

"LORD, WHAT ARE YOU DOING TO ME?" I cried from my heart. I stood there with tears coming to my eyes. "I'm running out of everything—money, food, everything. I won't be able to continue doing what you told me to do. I can't give food away if I don't have money to buy it with in the first place."

I thought of something St. Teresa of Avila once said to God when she was suffering. "If this is the way you treat your friends, Lord, no wonder you don't have many friends."

"Charlie, do you trust me?" was all I could hear the Lord saying.

"I have nothing to trust you with," I said.

"Good," the Lord answered. "Now you can really begin to trust me."

I looked at the table where those hungry young people were eating me out of house and home. One young man drank eight glasses of milk, ate two loaves of Italian bread, two steaks, and two seafood dinners.

"I'm not going to take this anymore," I decided when I heard him order another side dish of shrimp. "Lord," I said, "I just can't take it anymore."

I couldn't stand seeing those kids, those drunks and addicts, take away every last thing that I had worked so hard to obtain. I decided to go over to that table and run them off.

I just about flew out of the kitchen, I was so angry.

"Lord," I said. "I can't take it. Out they go."

"Don't you dare touch one of my children," he said.

I arrived at the table, my Bible in hand, with God's warning ringing in my ears. The street kids looked up at me curiously. I slammed my Bible down as hard as I could.

"I've come to tell you about Jesus," I said.

"O.K.," one of them answered. "We've never really heard much about Jesus. We'd like to hear about him."

"What? You would?"

I was flabbergasted. The Lord had turned my anger and frustration inside out so I would share his gospel with some young people who really needed to hear it. Each of those young people agreed that night to think about committing their lives to Jesus. Several of them said a prayer of commitment with me, and they were sincere. They had heard about God before, but they had not received the good news like they did that night. Right there in my restaurant God healed them from sicknesses, delivered them from drugs, and showed them the depth of his love. It was one of the most wonderful experiences of my life.

Two weeks later the young woman who had been drunk that night came back to the restaurant. She was wearing a dress, and the gaudy makeup she had worn was gone. She looked very pretty. She came in and asked me to read more Scripture to her.

I don't know what happened to the others. I never saw them again. I hope that they found a body of Christians so they could grow in the Christian life. That's what I encouraged them to do. It would have been nice to know what happened to them, but then I wasn't looking for success. I was just trying to follow the Lord one step at a time, trying to obey what I heard him say to me as soon as I understood what he was saying.

That episode was a turning point in my life. Through it God began to teach me how to love his people. I learned that it was the poor, the neglected, and the humble who were most interested in hearing about God's love. Most of my customers from the old days were not. They weren't interested in anything that was free, and they weren't interested in hearing about Jesus.

When I would approach a wealthy customer and say, "Brother, there's more to life than that bottle of wine," the response was usually, "Leave me alone, Charlie. I'm paying a good price for this meal."

But I couldn't stop sharing about the Lord. I felt that he wanted me to share the gospel with everyone I came in contact with, so I kept trying. Looking back I have to admit that that was no way to run a restaurant. Within about a year I had run off most of my original clientele. But I was still convinced that I was doing what God wanted me to do.

Some people think I went overboard in those days. But I don't think you can go overboard for Jesus. Everywhere Jesus went he caused a commotion, and so did the apostle Paul. Paul caused riots in city after city. Scripture said the world would hate me, but those who would believe in the Lord would love me and become my brothers and sisters.

After all my regular customers stopped coming and all my resources were gone, the Lord showed me that it was the needy people—the drug addicts, the prostitutes, the poor, and the neglected—who were the ones who would open their lives to God.

They would come to my wife and me asking for help. One girl told Jeanne that she wanted to find a respectable job. "I can't go back to the nightclub and sell myself to men anymore," she said. So we helped them find jobs and break out of bad relationships. We helped them find the Lord.

But they helped us too. And their help in the restaurant was invaluable, because thirty of my thirty-two employees quit when I took the prices off the menus. The two who remained were my mother-in-law, one of the best professional cooks in that part of Florida, and a very special waitress named Hilda

Wheelis. Hilda got so fired up with the love of the Lord that she stayed with me after the restaurant closed and I began a full-time ministry for Jesus.

After all the other employees had left, Hilda came to me and said, "If you can give away your food, I can give away my time." Since that day she has worked in this evangelistic ministry without any salary. Hilda is totally committed to the Lord. Why? Because she knows firsthand what a good God he is.

A few years before I met Hilda, she was a very sick woman. She had had stomach ulcers, colitis, arthritis, deterioration of the bones, and blood disease, all at the same time. She was put on a special diet to control the ulcers, but the food on this diet aggravated the colitis. The doctors prescribed aspirin for the arthritis, which then aggravated the ulcers. What's more, the bone condition was incurable and the blood disease was not responding to treatment. Hilda was in and out of a number of hospitals for several years, until the doctors finally gave up. They told her that she had reached the point of no return and that she would soon become completely incapacitated.

Fortunately, Hilda had a friend who insisted that she attend a healing service conducted by a Catholic priest, Father Robert DeGrandis. Hilda didn't believe in healing, but her friend persisted and she agreed to go. The service was in Mobile, Alabama, and the van they took to get there had improperly installed seats which aggravated Hilda's condition. By the time they arrived, she was in agony.

Hilda's friend helped her to the church and they took seats near the back. Hilda heard little of what the priest was saying because she was in such pain. After he finished his talk, however, she did hear him say that he was going to pray with every person present, beginning with those in pain. Hilda still did not believe in faith healing, but she raised her hand when he asked who was in pain at that moment.

When Father DeGrandis came to pray with Hilda, he

surprised her by telling her several things about her life that he simply could not have known had the Holy Spirit not revealed them to him. (This is a spiritual gift which is sometimes called "revelation" or "word of knowledge." It is like the gift of prophecy, where someone speaks to another on behalf of God.)

These personal revelations concerned things in Hilda's life that were causing her great emotional pain. Father DeGrandis told her that unless she forgave the people who were hurting her—including her own husband, who was living with another woman—she would never get well. He helped her understand that forgiveness is a decision, not a feeling. Hilda asked the Lord for the grace to decide to forgive her husband. Then Father DeGrandis prayed with her and the pain immediately left her body. God had healed her completely.

During the next few days Hilda began to try foods that she had been unable to eat for years. To her surprise, she could eat them without pain.

Later, when she returned to her doctor for tests that had been scheduled prior to the healing service, he told her to stop taking her medications. He could find no symptoms of her diseases.

As you might expect, Hilda was overjoyed at her healing and returned to the sessions conducted by Father DeGrandis to learn more about the Lord. Eventually, she told the Lord that she wanted to serve him in whatever way he wanted. She began going downtown every day after work to tell prostitutes, homosexuals, and others about the healing power of Jesus.

I got to know Hilda when she filled in from time to time for one of her daughters who was a waitress in my restaurant. Hilda knew all about my conversion to Christ, and when I dedicated the restaurant to the Lord, she came to work for me full-time. Knowing very well what God could do for needy people, she soon became a prayer warrior around the restaurant. When Hilda prayed with people, they were healed. She had strong faith and a big heart filled with love.

Hilda was also key in helping me establish a good relationship with Bishop Rene Gracida. Bishop Gracida was the bishop of my diocese and received all kinds of reports, most of them negative, about what I was doing. Hilda knew the bishop well and kept him informed about the ministry God was raising up among us. The bishop watched us carefully for five years, and then gave us his blessing.

Jeanne and I leaned heavily on Hilda during the three months after all our employees left us. It was an ordeal, and she was a pillar of strength for us. We ran out of just about everything, and people said terrible things about us. But as we started sharing Jesus with those who wanted him most, God himself began to help us.

At the end of those three months more than one hundred people were working at the restaurant. Most of them had come in off the street looking for a handout. Instead, they met Jesus Christ. They worked without pay and did just about everything. In fact, I hardly had to work myself. So I preached. Once every hour I took a microphone and invited anyone who wanted to give his or her heart to Jesus to pray with me.

It seems that there is a special relationship between food and Jesus. Jesus is the spiritual food we all so greatly need. That is why we are so moved by the account of the Last Supper, when Jesus gave his disciples the Bread of Life. That is why the Eucharist is the center of our faith and the high point of our worship.

I learned to take advantage of the relationship between Jesus and food. I'd take the microphone while my patrons were eating and say, "Dear brothers and sisters, I want to thank the one who allowed this meal to be possible for you. His name is Jesus." (Everyone would clap.) "Is there anyone here tonight who wants to give his life to Jesus?" Sometimes only a few people would respond, but at other times table after table of men and women would stand up and join me in a prayer of surrender to the Lord.

Many of the people who responded to my preaching were Catholics. I began to see ever more clearly that my mission in life was to win souls for the Lord as a Catholic evangelist.

In fact, I believe that that's the mission of every Catholic. As far as I am concerned, that is why we are on earth. We have been created, baptized, and blessed in abundance so we can win souls for the kingdom of our Lord Jesus Christ. The money we've made, the things we've done as artists, craftsmen, writers, or anything else won't matter when we get to heaven. What God is interested in is whether we have given his love to others.

At judgment, God is going to ask you a question: "Did you reach out to the poor, the hungry, the naked, the lonely with my love? What did you do to feed their empty stomachs and their empty spirits? Did you tell others about how I could help them?"

How will you answer?

It liberated me to discover what God thinks is important. I found that money and success and what people thought of me didn't matter at all. I was excited about serving the Lord. I'd get up in the morning jumping with joy, and I'd go to bed at night in the same way. Winning souls for the Lord is the most thrilling thing we can do.

It was thrilling, but it was also hard work. We'd be in the restaurant eighteen hours a day, feeding hungry people and ministering to everyone who was interested in Jesus Christ. My wife and I would drag ourselves out of the restaurant at one o'clock in the morning, absolutely exhausted, and walk home hand in hand. We didn't even own a car anymore, so we had to walk everywhere. But we were happy, and we'd sing Christian songs all the way home.

I had bad days too. Every day people would come into the

restaurant just to take advantage of the free food. I'd sometimes get upset with the Lord and cry out, "They're taking advantage of me!"

"Well," he would say, "they took advantage of me, too. Are you any better than I am?"

"But, Lord, they're ripping me off."

"They ripped me off, too," he answered.

"They're making fun of me."

"They made fun of me, too. They ridiculed me, Charlie, in ways they can never ridicule you."

"I know, but it hurts, Lord. It hurts."

Then the Lord would send in a whole gang of people who were drunk or high on drugs and say, "Charlie, if you can't love these children of mine, then you don't love me."

I knew I wanted to love the Lord. "Lord, teach me to love them. I have to know how to love these people. If that's what's required of me, I have to learn how."

And every time I prayed for it, he gave me the grace, not only to serve them gladly, but to witness to them about his love and mercy.

It took three years for the Lord to empty my life of selfishness, arrogance, pride, and self-reliance. Then he could use me for something else.

What a privilege to be used by God! What a thrill to be a Catholic lay evangelist. God has poured out his Spirit among his people. He has poured out his Spirit on the Catholic Church. We Catholics have the power of Almighty God living in us and the anointing of his Holy Spirit to witness for Jesus. We've got to get out and do it.

I am daily overwhelmed with the thought that God has given me the privilege of working with him. He has given me the greatest of all gifts—the ability to know him, to love him, and to serve him. He has given me eyes to see what he has done for me, what he is doing now, and what he will do forever. My life is eternal. My body will give out at the time of death, but my life will go on forever. Eternal life begins right now, today, when I obey the word of God which tells me to witness for Jesus Christ.

This is true for you as well. God calls all men and women to a life of service and love. It's the very purpose of life.

Perhaps you have not allowed Jesus to be the Lord of your life. Or you may have made a decision for him at one time but have not stuck with it. Perhaps you haven't experienced the great thrill of allowing the Holy Spirit to possess you, to own you, and to control you. If you haven't yet done it, I urge you to make a commitment to Jesus right now, right where you are. If you want to live for Jesus, turn to him by praying this simple prayer:

> Lord Jesus, by faith I turn to you now. I ask you to give me the joy and peace of knowing you. I want you to come into my life and be my Lord and Savior. I ask you to deliver me from the things of this world that stand between you and me. I need you, Lord Jesus. Fill me with your Holy Spirit that I may live my life as a child of God. I want to be free of sin, free of the attacks of Satan, and free of sickness. Come, Lord Jesus, be my Lord and Savior. Amen.

FOUR

Jeanne's Story

SO FAR YOU'VE BEEN READING about what God did for Charlie Osburn. I'd like to tell you what he did for me. I am Jeanne Osburn, Charlie's wife.

This is my story, too. When Charlie was experiencing the power of God in his life, so was I. But we went through some very tough years before the Lord rescued us both.

I have never forgotten that wonderful day, November 14, 1956, when I walked down the aisle of St. Michael's Church in Pensacola and pledged that I would spend the rest of my life with a man named Charlie Osburn. Many things had drawn me to Charlie since I had met him. One of the main reasons why I was confident about marrying him was that Charlie insisted that he would never drink alcohol. As a girl of nineteen I was very impressed with that conviction. I didn't know very many men of twenty-three who were not drinking.

When I stood next to Charlie on that special morning, I said that I would take him "for better or worse, till death do us part." Those were words of faith. I didn't know what was in store for us; no couple does when they marry. I didn't know it at the time, but what I was really saying was that I was going to love Charlie, no matter what it cost me.

And you know what happened? The man who said he would never drink began to drink. Then he became an alcoholic. As a result, my children and I were knocked around, used, and abused. That is the tragedy in many alcoholic homes.

During the worst days of his alcoholism Charlie ran around with the "jet set" of our town. Sometimes, while Charlie was out playing golf and having a good time, some of these "friends" would visit and encourage me to divorce him.

"Charlie is never going to change," they'd say. "You've got to teach him a lesson. Here's the name of a good lawyer. He'll take care of you."

It seemed strange that the very people my husband was wining and dining were the ones who were telling me to "teach him a lesson" by divorcing him. But I came very close to heeding their advice. I even went to see a lawyer and told him I wanted a divorce. When he had completed all the paperwork, I went to his office to sign it. But as I was riding up the elevator to the ninth floor to the lawyer's office, an inner voice said to me, "You're about to make a very big mistake."

By the time I walked into the lawyer's office I knew in my heart that I would never put my name on the divorce papers. I looked at the papers, and then at the lawyer and said, "I am really sorry that you've gone to all this effort, but this is the last place that I need to be this morning. I'm willing to pay you whatever you want for your efforts, but I'm not getting a divorce."

I wouldn't have said it this way at the time, but I made a decision to love Charlie just the way he was.

My mother met me at the door of the restaurant when I got back from the lawyer's office. As I greeted her, she asked what I had done. I smiled and said, "I'll tell you what I didn't do. I decided not to get a divorce."

Mama smiled at me and said, "Let me tell you something, Jeanne. You're a lot stronger than I am."

That's all she said. My mother never tried to tell me what to do. She respected me as an adult, and she loved me. Her loving support gave me a great deal of the strength that she admired so much.

One day when I got home from working at Charlie's restaurant, I found a note on a very small piece of paper. The note was written by my seventeen-year-old son, Craig. It said: "Mom, why can't we be a loving family?"

As I read that note I thought my heart was going to break. I realized how helpless I was. I had done everything I knew to improve our marriage and family. I had refrained from putting any kind of pressure on Charlie about how he spent his time or money. I had been very careful not to throw his misbehavior back at him by using angry words. I did whatever he wanted me to do, and I was always there for him when he wanted me. But none of it worked. I knew that night that I was totally helpless. When I went to bed, tears streaming down my face, I cried out, "Oh God, you've got to help me!"

A few nights later I was working in the restaurant when a large party came in and asked to dine in our banquet room. Among this group were three young men who were dressed exactly alike. We were almost ready to close when they came in, and I was so busy getting things closed up for the night that I didn't pay much attention to the group. I knew that the waitresses were taking good care of them.

I did notice, however, that there was a lot of singing coming from that room. I couldn't resist walking over and listening. It was the three young men (brothers, as I found out later) who were singing. They had wonderful voices. I mentioned to one of the waitresses that it would be nice if they would sing a song for us before they left.

A few minutes later she came to me and said, "They're ready to sing for us." So I rounded up all the waitresses, cooks, busboys, and dishwashers, and we gathered around their table. They sang a popular love song for us. It was very nice.

When they finished one of the young men looked at me

and said, "We don't mind singing these kinds of songs. But we really like to sing about Jesus."

When he mentioned the name "Jesus," I felt a sweet sensation in my body. It was a very strange feeling. I had never heard anyone mention the name of Jesus in a public place like that before, and it really did something for me.

We all thanked the singers and then got back to work. I told the waitress not to charge the three brothers for their meals. A short time later the party left, and we began finishing our chores so we could go home.

Not even a full minute after the singers' party had walked out the front door, the three brothers came back in. They had learned that I had paid for their dinners, and they wanted to thank me. I was standing behind the cashier's counter, and they encircled me and began singing the love song "I Believe." When they reached the line that says, "I believe that someday someone will come and show me the way," they changed the words and instead sang, "I believe that Jesus will come and show me the way."

It happened again! When they sang the name of Jesus, I felt as though a light bulb had been turned on in my heart.

They told me that they were called the Stone Brothers and were gospel singers from out of town. They said they would be in Pensacola again, performing at a particular church a few months later.

Because of the busyness of our lives and the increasing tension between Charlie and me, I forgot all about them. But one morning, as I was reading the newspaper, I came across an advertisement which announced that the Stone Brothers were coming to town for a concert. I asked Charlie to go to the church with me to see them, but initially he refused. I countered with a request that we at least stop by on our way home from the restaurant so I could run in and say hello to them. When he found out that the concert would be over by the time we arrived, he gave in and agreed to go.

When we got to the church, however, Charlie decided he

wanted to go in after all. When the brothers saw me, they sang another song for us. Charlie was flabbergasted by all the attention I was receiving. The Stone Brothers asked us to bring our entire family to the concert the next night and, to my surprise, Charlie agreed. But the next evening, when it was time to get ready to leave, Charlie was nowhere in sight. The children and I dressed and went to the church by ourselves. Seconds before the concert was to begin, Charlie slipped into a seat beside us.

The Stone Brothers came out and began to sing a number called "A Song Was Born When I Met Jesus." As I listened to them, I knew that something was indeed taking place inside me. During the concert, they sang, played trumpets, and offered testimonies about what the Lord had done for them. Then, towards the end, they invited everyone present who wanted to "make Jesus Lord of their lives" to come forward to be prayed with.

It was my first experience of an altar call. I didn't respond because I was afraid they would want me to join the Baptist Church. I knew, however, that I desperately needed to have Jesus in my life. I knew that I needed to surrender all my problems to him. Only he could help me. As one of the Stone Brothers recited "the sinner's prayer" for those who had gone forward, I followed along silently, and almost immediately a peace and security that I had never before known enveloped me. I was certain that Jesus had heard my plea, that he had entered my life in a new way.

After the concert the brothers came to our house for supper. As they stood in the kitchen, talking with me while I prepared the meal, I wanted to tell them what had happened to me during their concert. But I couldn't. I knew that Charlie wouldn't be able to handle any major change in my life, so I kept quiet about what I had experienced.

However, the Lord enabled me to love Charlie in a new way. I had never stopped loving my husband, no matter how cruel he had become. But God showed me how to love him in a spiritual way as well as in an emotional way. I was able to relate to Charlie without pressuring him, and I was freed of the anger and resentment that had burned in my heart. The Lord enabled me to forgive Charlie completely for the things he had done.

Our natural reaction when someone mistreats us is to resent both the action and the person. But the Lord wants us to let go of resentments and to forgive others. Unconditional forgiveness is the Christian way of life, and the Lord himself enables us to forgive this way. I'm not a great saint. The change in my attitude was a miracle of grace. I had to struggle and, at times, bite my tongue, but the Lord and his grace were there for me.

This was especially true on a Sunday a few weeks after the Stone Brothers' concert. It was our twentieth wedding anniversary, and Charlie had left town. He had decided to become a real estate agent in order to earn more money. The exam, which was being given in another part of Florida, was not until Monday, but Charlie had left on Saturday. I knew he had purposely planned to be away on our anniversary just to be spiteful. It hurt a great deal, and I had no one to turn to but Jesus.

While the children and I were at Mass that morning, my attention was continually drawn to the crucifix behind the altar. Each time I looked at it, it seemed to grow larger, and when it did, I experienced the love of Jesus flowing into my heart. Finally, after thinking about Charlie, I prayed, "Lord, I've tried to change my husband for twenty years, and I've been unable to do it. I've given my own life to you, and I give Charlie to you, too."

Just then the choir began singing a hymn called "Let There Be Peace on Earth," and the Lord's love and grace flooded my heart. It was a profound emotional and spiritual experience which I later realized was the baptism in the Holy Spirit. At the time, I only knew that the great Lord loved me enough to answer my prayer, and I was on cloud nine.

When I went forward to receive Jesus in the Eucharist, the Lord gave me a greater love for Charlie. I knew that this love could help create an opening for God to begin working in Charlie's life, too. I returned to my seat and began to cry. Jesus had worked a great healing in me and I wanted to tell someone. How I wished I could go home and tell Charlie!

As soon as we got home I phoned Charlie at his motel. When he answered I said: "Honey, I want you to know that I love you just the way you are and that it doesn't matter to me where you go or how long you stay or who you go with. I'll be waiting for you." Then I hung up.

Charlie says that he just stood there in the motel room not knowing what to do. When he had heard my voice on the phone, he had expected me to tell him that he was a sorry excuse for a man and that three lawyers would be waiting for him when he returned. He would have known how to handle that. But he didn't know how to handle love or how to respond to it.

That was November 14, 1976. The following February 8, Charlie Osburn, the "wild man of Warrington," the man who could never change, the man that I "had to teach a lesson to," went down on his knees with Father Jim Smith, surrendered his life to the Lord Jesus, and asked for the infilling of God's Holy Spirit.

That was only the beginning of Charlie's process of conversion. Other wonderful things needed to happen before he could become the loving husband and marvellous minister of God's word that he is today. But they did happen. Charlie was indeed capable of changing, and the Holy Spirit was up to the task of changing him. In time our marriage was put in right order. It was a long, sometimes difficult process. Charlie tended to be obstinate and impulsive, and I sometimes tried to manipulate him. We had to learn how to continually forgive one another. We also had to learn how to pick ourselves up after we had fallen and start following after Jesus again. But we persisted and God continued to perform his miracles of grace and love in our lives. Charlie and I fell in love with each other all over again. And not only were we in love with each other, we were in love with everyone else, too!

Now these two Osburns, who were in love with each other and on fire for Jesus, had five other Osburns in the house to consider. We had taught our five children how to live well in the world. We taught them how to make it on their own, how to watch out for "number one," how to party, and so forth. They knew how to get on in life. But now their parents started living like Christians.

Three of them scattered. One son got married and joined the Air Force, all on the same day. Our daughter Regina was married. Craig moved out and a short while later was married. Suddenly we found ourselves with only two children left at home, Doug and Amy. At that time Doug was the most rebellious child I had ever seen. He was so full of resentment that he wouldn't even speak to anyone else in the house. He just walked passed us as fast as he could without saying a word.

One night Charlie was out speaking to a prayer group. He called me afterwards. "Honey," he said, in an excited voice, "praise the Lord! How are things going?"

"Do you really want to know how things are going back here?" I thought.

"What's wrong with you?" he asked. "I don't hear that joy in your voice."

I then told him all about Doug. Charlie's words to me were, "I want you to love Doug just the way he is. Don't expect him to do anything for you."

The next evening Doug came to me and asked for two dollars. I had two dollars, but that was all I had. I didn't respond immediately because I was busy washing the evening dishes. I then forgot all about my son's request and left the house with my daughter Amy.

I had been driving for about fifteen minutes when I remembered that I had not given Doug the two dollars. As I turned the car around, Amy said, "Mom, you're not really driving all the way back home just to give Doug two dollars."

"I sure am," I said, and hurried back home.

As I pulled into the carport Doug pushed the door open as hard as he could and said, "It's too late; I don't want your money any more."

I could sense what Amy was thinking. She wanted to strike out at her ungrateful brother. Still smiling I put the car in reverse, pulled out into the street, and said to Amy, "We have to love Doug just the way he is."

The next morning Doug passed me in the hall.

"Doug," I said, "your two dollars is on the kitchen counter. Please forgive me for the resentment I had in my heart for you last night."

That night as I was coming out of my bedroom, Doug met me in the hallway. He reached over and kissed me on the cheek. "Mom," he said, "I want you to know how much I love you."

That was the beginning of a new and open relationship between Doug and me. There has been no more rebellion, no more resentment. But it came at a high cost. I had to die to myself and reach out to love him with God's love.

Amy, who was twelve years old when Jesus came into our home, also changed a great deal. She was accustomed to getting whatever she wanted, whenever she wanted it. We raised her that way. Then her parents changed, and she changed right along with us. Because of the changes at the restaurant, we didn't have reliable income. We no longer had the money to get her everything she wanted, although, for the first time in her life, we were able to give her all the love she wanted and needed.

One day she came to me and said, "Mom, I know you don't have the money for this. But do you suppose that if I asked Jesus, he would send us some money so I can get a pair of shoes? I really need them."

It was all I could do to keep from bursting into tears. My

little girl had been hurt deeply in her life, but God had healed her. Her simple, childlike request really touched me. We prayed right there, and in a few days she was able to get the new shoes she needed. Today, Amy is a strong, faithful, young Christian woman. A whole book could be filled with the stories of the people she has been able to help because she experienced the love of Jesus in her life.

As Charlie and I learned how to take seriously the words of the gospel and the teachings of the Catholic Church, our children and other relatives saw our sincerity and our dedication and responded to it. Time and again we asked each of our children to forgive us for the mistakes we had made, the many times we had failed to love them and care adequately for their needs. The healing took years and, in fact, is still going on. But God continues to be faithful.

As things changed within our house, they also began to change at our restaurant, Mama Nunnari's.

The first thing that changed was the ownership and the name. Charlie and I ran the place before. Now we decided that Jesus would run it. We renamed the restaurant "Good News Restaurant" because we decided to use it to tell everyone we could what wonderful things Jesus had done for us.

We encountered problems as soon as other Christians around town found out what we were doing. We served alcohol in our bar, and they said, "You can't possibly be a Christian and love Jesus like you say you do when you are operating a lounge in your restaurant." This came as a surprise to us. We hadn't realized how strongly many Christians feel about drinking alcohol. Things were simple at the time. We just knew that Jesus had come in and healed our marriage and put a deep love in our hearts for everyone we met.

I remember hearing Charlie on the phone one night with a woman who was complaining about the lounge. He didn't understand why she was upset, but ended the conversation by saying, "Sister, if I'm doing something wrong, pray for me."

The following week Charlie heard a radio preacher, Pastor Billy Smith, discussing the Letter to the Romans. The preacher read the passage: "You should resolve to put no stumbling block or hindrance in your brother's way" (Rom 14:13). Charlie realized that even though he differed from many Christians in his view on the righteousness of alcohol, serving alcohol in the lounge was clearly a stumbling block. As is his habit, Charlie acted immediately. He called and asked me to gather everyone who worked at the restaurant together for a meeting.

When all of our employees were assembled, Charlie looked at each person and said, "I want you to know that there will never be any kind of beverage sold in this restaurant except coffee, tea, soft drinks, and water." Then he explained why.

The lounge closed, and all but two of our employees quit. Before long, all of our regular customers also left, and we ended up with a wonderful restaurant but no one to serve. So we turned the restaurant into a Christian supper club, which drew Christians from around town.

Then the Lord led Charlie to take the prices off the menu, and the Christians stopped coming. They found it too confusing to have to figure out how much to pay for their food.

During all this time of the agony and the ecstasy of trying to live the gospel, there was one great woman who stood quietly in the background, praying with all her might. That woman was my mother, Janet Nunnari.

Mama and her brothers had operated a number of restaurants in the Pensacola area for decades. In fact, Charlie and I got into the restaurant business because of their success. We took the business over from them and, even though we changed it quite a bit, we probably would not have been successful if it hadn't been for their reputation and my mother's ability to cook.

During all our years of troubled marriage, she stood by us.

She was our chief cook and she never missed a day. Even after Charlie took the prices off the menus she stayed with us, cooking for the down-and-outers and watching forty years of hard work in the restaurant business go down the drain. When we stopped paying our employees, she continued to work, happy to do so. My father also came in every morning to help with the clean-up work.

I believe that Charlie and I were able to grow as quickly as we did because of my parents' faithfulness to us and because of their prayers. Many times it was very hard for them to watch what was happening. But they kept quiet, prayed for us, and supported us as best they could. Their love was rewarded. They saw our family turned around, and they saw the fruit of the evangelization that went on in the Good News Restaurant. That was enough for them. They were very happy for us.

Eventually, the only people who came to the restaurant were street people and down-and-outers, people from the highways and the byways. We were living out the Scripture that says, "Don't give to those from whom you can expect a return. Rather, give to those who can't pay you back." (See Lk 6:32-35.)

Not long after we made this change, the doors of the restaurant swung open and a man stuck his head in.

"Lady," he said to me, "is this where you can come and get a steak for a quarter?"

"Oh, Lord," I thought, "what are you doing to us?"

One night Charlie was so upset that he went into the men's restroom and cried out, "Oh, God, help me!" At the same time, I was in the ladies' room saying, "Jesus, what are you doing?"

Charlie and I soon realized how helpless we were. We still held on to the things we had accumulated, and that selfishness was slow to leave. The whole process of letting go was very uncomfortable, but we learned an important lesson. The Lord showed us that we were to love the poor and the weak and the neglected. We were to love them right into the kingdom of God. If they were to be evangelized, if they were to discover that they were sons and daughters of the living God, they had to experience love from us so that they could recognize God's love when he showed it to them.

One couple used to come in frequently, and God used them to show me where my heart was. They were always on drugs or alcohol and ordered the best dinners on the menu. Every time they came, Hilda would tell them about the Lord, but it didn't seem to sink in.

One night, as I watched them walk across the parking lot towards the front door, I said to myself, "Lord, no. Not them again. I can't take this anymore, Lord." I put my head down on the counter and said, "Lord, you are going to have to give me your love, because I have no more love to give."

Miraculously, God did. He changed my heart and let me love not only that couple, but all who came into the restaurant.

One evening Charlie said that the Lord wanted him to go out among the customers and share about Jesus. He did. Then he invited those who wanted Jesus to be the Lord of their lives to come pray with him. One of the first ones up was Sheila, the woman that I had had so much trouble with. She stood next to Charlie, a big smile on her face, and she gave him a kiss. Then a young man came forward while I was playing the piano. He looked familiar, but I didn't recognize him. Then I looked into his eyes and realized it was the young man who came in with Sheila almost every day. He had had hair down to his waist, and he always wore a big old marijuana belt buckle. Tonight he was dressed well and his hair was cut shorter than Charlie's. That night they both surrendered their lives to the Lord and God allowed me to witness it. He had truly answered my prayers!

Months later Sheila came over to me and said, "Jeanne, can I say a prayer with you?"

"Sure, Sheila," I replied.

She reached for my hand and prayed: "Father, I want to thank you for Charlie and Jeanne loving me, when I didn't even know you existed."

What is evangelization? It's loving people into the kingdom of God. That is what we had done by giving food and attention to these young people, even though at the time we didn't fully realize it. We just obeyed God as he spoke to us.

Great things began happening to Charlie and me when we began to pray for God's love and for his grace. He healed our marriage, healed our relationship with each of our children, and called us to spread the good news of salvation to those who need to hear it. We are rich. We need nothing more.

What God did for me, he'll do for anyone. He will do it for you. God gave me grace and mercy and riches beyond anything I could imagine, and he's eager to do this for everyone. The Bible says God is no respecter of persons. The first step to a fuller life in Christ is to believe in your heart that he loves you. Then be willing to share that love with others. The gospel of Jesus is a message of love, mercy, and forgiveness. When we decide to accept Jesus, to receive his love and to live for him, we have no choice but to love, to be merciful, to forgive.

One of my favorite evangelists says that when we receive the good news, we have to become good news. How true that is!

For the past several years Charlie and I have been travelling all over the United States, loving people into the kingdom of God. And the point I stress is that we must love the members of our families and love them with God's love. "If you can't love your family, whom you can see, how can you love God, whom you can't see?" (See 1 Jn 4:20-21.)

So, love your spouse. Love your children. They are sons and daughters of God. And with God it's possible to love them. With him all things are possible.

As I look back on more than twenty-five years of marriage with the man to whom I pledged my life, I am filled with gratitude for Charlie. He taught me how to love God. He taught me how to walk in faith and to trust in the Lord.

One night he was preaching and he said, "I don't trust my wife." What he meant was that we are not to put our trust in people. We love people and put our trust in God.

FIVE

The Bishops' Call to Lay People

ONE DAY MY GRANDDAUGHTER MEGAN, who was two-and-a-half years old at the time, was taken to the doctor for a check-up. One of the first things the doctor said to her was, "Megan, I'm going to check your heart."

"That's where Jesus lives," she told him. "Jesus lives in my heart. He loves me."

That's incredible—two-and-a-half years old and already witnessing for Jesus. Why does she do it? Because her parents, with a little prompting from granddad, have taught her that she is a child of King Jesus. That little girl knows exactly who she is.

The same cannot be said for most Christians. Unfortunately, most Christians don't realize who they are.

A few weeks after this incident, my wife took Megan on a shopping trip to a large department store. A woman shopping near them was pushing a screaming baby in a stroller. This poor harried mother could not get the child to stop crying.

After a short while, Megan quietly slipped out of her grandmother's grasp. Suddenly, the crying stopped. Jeanne looked around, and there was Megan, her hands on the baby's head, praying in tongues. Whatever had been annoying that child vanished with Megan's prayer, and everyone continued peacefully with their shopping.

Megan was not really an extraordinary two-year-old. She simply said and did the things that all Christians—children and adults alike—should say and do. She has known, from her earliest childhood, who she is. Anyone who asked Megan at that young age, "Who are you, Megan?" received a direct reply: "I am a child of God."

When we know who we are and what our purpose in this life is, everything else suddenly begins to make sense. We begin to understand why we are on this earth and what we are supposed to do while we are here. And most Christians do have some idea about the meaning of life. They know that they are supposed to believe in God, attend church, and do good deeds once in a while, in order to go to heaven when they die.

But most Christians to whom I minister do not comprehend the significance of the things in which they believe. The majority are not alcoholic scoundrels like I used to be. Yet they do not act like people who know who they are. Their knowledge of God and Jesus is frequently limited. They attend church because they know they should. They try to be honest, truthful, and fair in dealing with others because they know that these are the "right things to do." They contribute money to their church and to collections for the poor because they know this pleases God.

There is nothing wrong with any of these things. They are a good beginning in our walk with Christ. But they only scratch the surface of the Christian life. As responses to the grace and mercy that God has poured out on us in Christ Jesus and his church, they are simply inadequate. Christian life is more than a system of intellectual beliefs. It is a thrilling daily walk with the most wonderful, the most powerful, the most appealing person in the entire universe. It is tremendously exciting to discover who you are, where you came from, and where you are going. And when you walk in this knowledge, you walk with greater boldness, with more zip in your step. You enjoy true peace and the conviction that every day of your life has a real purpose.

Many Christians have given their hearts and lives to the Lord and yet do not experience this kind of assurance. They are burdened with problems. They are afraid to talk to their friends and neighbors about the Lord. They are often angry or impatient with their spouse and children. Material things still tug at their hearts and distract them from serving God.

Well, it's really not as hard to change as we often think. We need to start behaving in a new way. When we do, God gives us the grace to make it. The first step is to read and to pray. Find out who you are and what God wants you to do with your life. A great deal of godly wisdom which will help you is contained in the gospels and in the Second Vatican Council's Decree on the Apostolate of Lay People. After some study and prayer, it's time to take action. Talk to your pastor, or to an active Christian lay person that you admire. They're sure to have advice for you. But don't neglect the gospels.

The gospels tell us about the life and teachings of Jesus. They reveal to us a faith in which to believe and a teaching to follow. But there is much more to the gospels than most of us realize. Jesus was excited about who he was and excited about his mission. When I read the gospels, I can just hear him saying, "Glory, hallelujah! I've come to do a work. I'm here to glorify my Father." I can just imagine him shouting with happiness as he preached the good news, thrilled when someone embraced his message. Jesus was enthusiastic.

The men and women who met Jesus, who believed in his teaching, were completely changed by that experience. The gospels tell us about many of them. Peter was an uneducated fisherman, headstrong and chicken-hearted. But Jesus changed him. Mary Magdalene was a prostitute. Jesus changed her. The sick, the blind, the poor in faith—Jesus changed them all.

Yet they had to do something in order to be changed. They

had to meet Jesus, listen to his teaching, and believe in him and his words. When they did, he revolutionized their lives. There was new meaning and purpose. And these people were happy! Thrilled with what Jesus had done for them, they eagerly shared that good news with others.

The gospels and the Decree on the Apostolate of Lay People tell us we are to be like that, too. We are to meet Jesus personally and give our lives to him. We are to live as sons and daughters of God. We are part of Jesus' mission to save the human race and should actively work with him to bring truth, joy, and peace to the men and women he brings to us. It could not be more clear. I know exactly who I am and so should you.

God has chosen each of us, no matter how unlikely we seem, to be an important part of Jesus' mission in the world. God is not looking for a genius. All he wants is a willing heart. And all we need to do is say, "Yes, Lord, pull me through that knothole. Strip off my pride, Lord. Remove my selfishness. Give me a spirit of love, and let me see people the way you see them."

When Catholic lay people, men and women, boys and girls, take on this attitude, we'll see this wonderful church evangelize the entire world! What could be more exciting than that? There are millions of Peters, millions of Mary Magdalenes, millions of Charlie Osburns out there who are starving for the good news of Jesus Christ. They will jump for joy when you tell them about him. But you first have to know who you are. Then you have to know *how* to tell them.

The first thing that we, as Catholic lay people, must recognize is that it is up to us. We can choose to be part of Jesus' work, our true calling, or to ignore it. We can sit back and leave the church's work to the priests and nuns, where we may have for years assumed it belonged. It's easy to assume that. It is also a great mistake. *We* are the church—men and women, boys and girls. We are supposed to do the work of Jesus. We can't do the priest's work, of course. He celebrates the liturgy for us, administers the sacraments, leads us to Jesus who gives us the grace to serve God. That's the priest's role. But one of the biggest problems I have encountered in parish after parish is that everyone is waiting on the priest—waiting for him to attend prayer meetings, waiting for him to be more "spiritual." People think they need to go somewhere else "to be fed."

Many good people have been hurt because their commitment to Jesus and to his work has not been well received in their parish. But Jesus doesn't want them to "go somewhere else to be fed." When the disciples brought food to Jesus after he had been talking with the woman at the well (the one who had had five husbands), Jesus told them, "I have food to eat of which you do not know.... Doing the will of him who sent me and bringing his work to completion is my food" (Jn 4:32-33).

Jesus had been eating of the food of the Spirit. So can we. When we begin eating the food of the Spirit, we'll begin to do the work that Jesus did.

We can only do this work when we know who we are (sons and daughters of the living God), where we are headed (to a glorious reward in heaven), and how we're going to get there (by doing the work Jesus wants us to do).

Scripture clearly says that God has put us all under authority. The bishops are the authority in the Catholic Church, so when I began my walk with Jesus I wanted to know what my bishops were saying about how I was to conduct my life as a layman.

Before I began reading the Bible and the documents of Vatican II, all I knew about authority was what I had learned through my business. I had thirty-two employees under my authority. I told them to be at work at a certain time and they were there. When I told them to go home, they went. They were under my authority and they obeyed.

As Catholics we are under the authority of our bishops. Therefore, I wanted to know what they wanted me to do as a

Catholic layman. I had discovered who I was in Jesus. Now I needed to know how I fit into the body. I had already spoken with my pastor and read things my own bishop had written. But I had no idea that the bishops of the church had written a document describing precisely what they expect of me. I began to find out one night in San Antonio, Texas. I'd been invited to San Antonio to present the story of my conversion at some Catholic prayer meetings there. After one of these meetings I returned to the apartment of a friend, when Jim Manning, a leader of one of the prayer groups, handed me a copy of the documents of Vatican II.

"Charlie," he said, "you need to read this."

"No," I said, "it's too thick."

"Look," he answered, "I've already got it underlined for you. Just read the parts I've underlined."

"That's not so hard," I said. And it wasn't. In fact, it was easy to read what the 2,500 bishops assembled in Rome for the Council had to say to us, the church. They weren't just talking to each other. They weren't just talking to the priests and nuns. They were talking to me, Charlie Osburn, a layman. And they had some great things to say.

God turned on a light in my life. I had gone through three years of humiliation in my restaurant, three years of being taken advantage of and not knowing what was going to happen from one day to the next. I thought I couldn't go any further. I'd lost all my friends, all my customers, all my employees except for two. The Lord had told me to give the food away, and so my restaurant was full of alcoholics and drug addicts. It is true that I experienced great joy when we led a lost soul to the Lord. But those successes were few and far between. Most of the people who came into my restaurant didn't want Jesus. They just wanted to freeload. They would take my food and then laugh at me, sometimes right in my face. They called me a fool, and it was humiliating.

I had believed so much in this ministry to the needy that, after closing the lounge, I had the bar ripped out and turned the room into a dormitory for homeless men. We installed a shower, put in sixteen cots, and began to take people in. Some nights there were more men than cots, so we'd bring the extras home. Many times Jeanne would pin a note to the back door, telling our children to be careful where they walked when they came in the house. We didn't want them to step on a man in a sleeping bag on the dining room floor.

Each morning I conducted a Bible study for these men and prayed with those who were interested. Then they'd work around the restaurant, or go out and look for jobs. Our shelter became famous. Sometimes the sheriff's deputies would stop by with a carload of drifters and drop them off for a good night's sleep and a couple of hot meals.

One Sunday morning when Jeanne and I arrived at the restaurant, we saw a beat-up old station wagon parked out front. Inside were three ragged men. "The cops told us to come here," they said. "They told us you'd give us something to eat and take care of us."

One of these was a huge man, the biggest man I'd ever seen. He owned nothing but the clothes on his back, and they weren't in very good shape. We had clothing available for people who needed it, but we had nothing that would fit this man. So Jeanne called up a seamstress we knew and asked her to make this fellow some clothes.

A few nights later, I woke up in the middle of the night and began to pray. While I was talking with the Lord, he told me to give our car to our large friend. I woke Jeanne up to tell her this news. "Praise the Lord," she said. But, she admitted later, she didn't mean it.

The next morning I told the man that God wanted me to give him our car. He said that he couldn't accept it, and I was relieved. I really didn't want to give away our only car. But one morning, while Jeanne and I were praying, we were both overcome with the conviction that we had to give up the car. The issue wasn't the car itself, but our desire to cling to this possession rather than to the Lord. We hurried over to the restaurant and told our friend that God really wanted us to give him our car.

He was doing some work in the parking lot when we spoke with him. "No one has ever given me anything in my entire life," he said, and he fell down on the pavement and began to cry.

He never did accept the car, but he did come to believe in the Lord and began to live like a Christian. He stayed with us for several weeks and then left. He continued to drift around the area, but with a new purpose. Instead of stealing to earn his livelihood, he found odd jobs and used most of the money he earned to repay people he had stolen from in the past. He kept in touch with us for years, assuring us that he was getting his life together with the help of the Lord.

Yet despite successes like these, I was still a confused man. I had lost everything, and God was stripping away my pride as well. It was at this point of utter weakness and hopelessness that I read this:

> The laity are made to share in the priestly, prophetic, and kingly office of Christ; they have, therefore, in the church and in the world, their own assignment in the mission of the whole people of God. In the concrete, their apostolate is exercised when they work at the evangelization and sanctification of men.

This amazing statement is from the bishops' Decree on the Apostolate of Lay People. The bishops say that the laity have a share of Jesus' ministry. We are priests, prophets, and kings. We have an assignment, a mission—to bring other men and women to Jesus Christ and his church ("evangelization and sanctification"). That's a big job, and a big responsibility. And I had never heard about it.

When I read that statement, I felt as though, like St. Paul, I had had my sight restored. Paul received back his physical sight, but, even more important, he received spiritual vision. The Lord told him what to do. And now, through the bishops' decree, the Lord had told me what to do.

For forty-three years I had sought notoriety in the world, never realizing what my place in it was meant to be. The council document opened a whole new world for me. I realized that I didn't have to be a mayor, or a successful businessman, or anything else, to be happy and fulfilled in life. I had been baptized into the church. I was to be an apostle of Jesus Christ and to cooperate with him in his "priestly, prophetic, and kingly office." I was anointed, filled with the Holy Spirit, so I could preach the gospel of Jesus.

This is not just true for me, but for all of us. We are all supposed to spread the gospel of Jesus Christ. You don't have to have a preaching ministry to be an evangelist. You don't have to appear on television or write books. All you have to do is to tell other people about God's love revealed in the person of Jesus Christ.

God sent his love, his Word, his own Son to the earth to evangelize the world in a spirit of love. His love binds people together. His love heals. We need not be afraid of sharing the gospel. When we share the gospel, we share the love of God, and Jesus himself will be there, loving that person. We say a few words; Jesus does the hard part.

Of course, sometimes we'll be rejected. But most of us have said or done things before which haven't been well received. It will happen here, too. We just need to remember who we are (sons and daughters of God), why we're here (to be his apostles), and that God himself is with us.

We, the laity, have an obligation to evangelize. Consider these statements from the council's decree:

> From the fact of their union with Christ the head flows the laymen's right and duty to be apostles. Inserted as they are in the Mystical Body of Christ by baptism and

> strengthened by the power of the Holy Spirit in confirmation, it is by the Lord himself that they are assigned to the apostolate. If they are consecrated a kingly priesthood and a holy nation, it is in order that they may in all their actions offer spiritual sacrifices and bear witness to Christ the world over.
>
> Between the members of this body there exists, further, such a unity and solidarity (see Eph 4:16) that a member who does not work at the growth of the body to the extent of his possibilities must be considered useless both to the church and to himself.

The bishops clearly say that God himself assigns to each of us a practical role in the church's mission of spreading the kingdom of God throughout the world. Furthermore, any "member who does not work at the growth of the body to the extent of his possibilities must be considered useless both to the church and to himself."

"Useless." If we aren't involved in an apostolic work that helps the church grow by evangelizing new members into the church and by sanctifying current members, we are useless. And not just to the church, but to ourselves as well. Spiritual activity, apostolic work, ministry. Those aren't just nice words. They are what life is all about.

The bishops continue:

> The Holy Spirit sanctifies the People of God [that's you and me] through the ministry [of the clergy] and the sacraments. However, for the exercise of the apostolate he gives the faithful special gifts besides.

Then the decree refers to this scripture: "To each person the manifestation of the Spirit is given for the common good" (1 Cor 12:7).

The reason we can be useful is that the gifts of the Holy Spirit are ours for the asking:

> From the reception of these charisms [gifts of the Holy Spirit], even the most extraordinary ones, there arises for each of the faithful the right and duty of exercising them in the church and in the world for the good of men and the development of the church, of exercising them in the freedom of the Holy Spirit who "breathes where he wills." (Jn 3:8)

God makes demands of us, but he gives us the spiritual gifts we need to meet them. What more do we need to know? Yet, the lay people in a typical Catholic parish on Sunday morning don't display much enthusiasm. We act as if God hasn't done anything yet. The bishops warn us about being useless. Jesus warns us too: "Every tree that does not bear good fruit is cut down and thrown in the fire" (Mt 7:19).

Jesus wants us to bear good fruit. He wants us to love, serve, evangelize, and sanctify unbelievers and one another. He gives us the gifts and the power of the Holy Spirit to do these things. And, through the bishops of Vatican II, he tells us how to live a life of Christian service. The Decree on the Apostolate of Lay People tells us who we are, what the Lord and the church expect of us, how we fit into the body, and how we should exercise our gifts and talents. It is, very simply, a complete course in Christian life. Read it, study it, apply it, and your everyday Christian life will take off like a rocket.

God has worked a miracle in my life. I used to be a lover of things and a user of people. Now I am a user of things and a lover of people. I'm not boasting about Charlie Osburn. I'm boasting about God! And he wants to work a similar kind of miracle in the lives of every man and woman on the face of the earth. You and I are the keys. God wants to use us in his work.

We are often told to respond to the world situation with anger, judgment, and condemnation. Well, the world *is* in terrible shape. It may be worse than ever before in history. But anger, judgment, and condemnation are not the answer.

One reason the world is in the state it's in is because we Christians are not doing our job. Most of us are not loving, evangelizing, and serving. If we were, the world would be different. And if every Roman Catholic would begin to do what the bishops tell us in the Decree on the Apostolate of Lay People, the world would improve significantly in just a short time.

Let's heed what the bishops say to us:

> The council, then, makes to all the laity an earnest appeal in the Lord to give a willing, noble and enthusiastic response to the voice of Christ, who at this hour is summoning them more pressingly, and to the urging of the Holy Spirit. It is the Lord himself, by this council, who is once more inviting all the laity to unite themselves to him ever more intimately, to consider his interests their own, and to join in his mission as savior. It is the Lord who is again sending them into every town and every place where he himself is to come. He sends them on the church's apostolate . . . where they are to show themselves his cooperators, doing their full share continually in the work of the Lord, knowing that in the Lord their labor cannot be lost.

We must have an intimate, everyday relationship with Jesus and view everything that happens in our lives as an opportunity to witness to someone about his love. Life really changes when you begin to do that.

The bishops' document is a mandate for every one of us. Twenty-five hundred bishops, speaking under the inspiration of the Holy Spirit and under the authority of Jesus Christ, have told us to preach and teach the gospel. So, let's do it!

SIX

Taking to the Air

SIX MONTHS AFTER I RECOMMITTED MY LIFE TO JESUS CHRIST as a Catholic layman, Father Jim Smith, the priest who had led me to the Lord, suggested that I enter our diocese's permanent deacon training program.

Permanent deacons are Catholic men ordained into the diaconate—the first step towards priesthood—with the understanding that they will not be ordained priests. Most permanent deacons are married men. They serve the church in a number of ways, usually by assisting parish priests. Deacons are able to do most of what a priest does, except celebrate the Eucharist or hear confessions.

Father Smith thought that the diaconate would provide a good place for me to serve because God was clearly calling me to be a Catholic evangelist. I thought very highly of Father Smith and of his relationship with the Lord, so I agreed to apply. The screening board selected me to enter the program with about two dozen other men.

I applied myself to the studies of the training program, but most of my spiritual growth was occurring at the restaurant. It was during my second year as a diaconal candidate that we took the prices off our menus and began to give away our food. This began quite a stir among the people in the diaconate program and in my parish, as well as among my friends and neighbors. They could not understand why I would do such a thing. One day in church I was even the subject of a sermon, in which the priest accused me of being on an ego trip.

All this came as quite a shock to me because I thought I was only doing what Jesus wanted. The greatest shock came at a meeting my wife and I had with the director of the diaconate program. We had been meeting with him regularly so he could evaluate my progress in the studies. And, since Jeanne and I spent most of our time at the restaurant, we always met there.

Father came in and we all sat down around a table. He looked at me and said, "Charlie, you're turning people off with your preaching. We can't attract any new men to the diaconate program because you're scaring them away."

I was stunned! Were people actually not entering the diaconate simply because Charlie Osburn was in it?

Father said, "Charlie, I want you to slow down. You're going too fast. You've got to stop turning people off."

Well, ever since I had given my life to Jesus and experienced the baptism in the Holy Spirit, I wanted to share it. I had problems, even some anguish over things the Lord told me to do, but I had experienced the wonderful love of Jesus, and I wanted to share it. Why shouldn't everyone experience the joy of the Lord? If the Lord would give himself to me, he'd give himself to anyone. And that was the message I knew God wanted me to share with people. Now, I happen to be an exuberant man. I like to shout. So when Jesus came into my life and filled me with his joy, I began shouting "Glory! Hallelujah!" everywhere I went.

One day I asked Father Smith to go on the radio and tell all the listeners what he had told me about Jesus. "I'll pay for the time," I said. "You just explain to them the love and mercy of the Lord, the same way you explained it to me."

"Charlie," he answered, "I'm not comfortable doing that. I can witness one to one, but I wouldn't do well on the radio."

"Okay," I said. "If you can't do it, how about me? Will you

support me if I start an evangelistic radio program for Catholics?"

He did and I did. So, while I was involved in the diaconate training program, I preached for thirty minutes every day on a radio show. I'd open with "Glory to God! Hallelujah! This is your Catholic lay evangelist bringing you another exciting day in the life of our Lord Jesus."

The response was great. The program was the station's biggest hit and one of the most popular radio shows in town. One day a woman called and said, "I tuned in to your show while I was driving to the grocery store, and I just couldn't turn the radio off. I sat there in the hot sun and listened until the program was over."

I had received many calls like that, so when the director of the diaconate told me I was turning people off, it was a real blow. I didn't want to turn people off. I wanted to turn them on to Jesus and his love for them. Shortly after our meeting ended, I became physically ill and went home to bed. The next morning I went to the restaurant, but after an hour I went home sick again. I had never been this ill in my life.

I prayed all afternoon. "Lord," I asked, "what am I going to do? Show me what to do."

At about five in the afternoon I went back to the restaurant. The first thing I noticed as I walked in the door was a piece of blue paper on the counter. I picked it up and saw that it was addressed to me. I was so dejected I stuck it in my pocket and sat down at a table. After a while I pulled the note out of my pocket and read it. It had been written by a lady in the prayer group Jeanne and I attended. What I read was an amazing answer to the anguished prayers I had prayed all day long:

"Dear Charles, I've been meaning to tell you this for a long time. You cannot turn off those that are turned on. And those that are turned off have already turned away."

That's it, I thought. That's the answer! It's like turning off a light switch. If I depress a light switch and hold it down for fifty years, the lights will never be more turned off than they were when I depressed the switch. When they're off, they're off. But if I were to move my finger and put a little pressure in the opposite direction, the lights would go on.

I realized then that I could not turn someone off. No evangelist can. We can't turn people off—they turn themselves off. But if we talk and preach long enough, some of those turned off will turn themselves back on. They'll receive the light of Jesus into their lives and know the same joy I do. I've heard many testimonies by people who said they were turned off, and then, when the time was right for them, they were turned on.

Now, even though I couldn't turn people off, I could anger them. I upset quite a few apple carts. But so did Jesus. And so did the apostle Paul. They were both driven out of several towns. Yet there were always a few people who followed them even out of town because they'd been turned on. They believed the message and received the joy of the Lord into their lives. It's the same today. If you're a shouter, go ahead and shout. If you're a soft-spoken person, share the gospel that way. The important thing is that, just like Jesus, we share the gospel and the joy of knowing the Lord at every opportunity.

I didn't want to alienate anyone, so I made a sincere effort to follow the directives laid down for me by the director of the diaconate program. I had to. God had placed him in a position of authority over me, and God expected me to obey him.

I finished the training for the diaconate, and Jeanne and I went to see the bishop to decide whether or not I should be ordained a permanent deacon. Bishop Gracida told us that he didn't think I should be ordained. He believed that God could use me better as a lay evangelist. Jeanne and I agreed, so I withdrew from the program.

At that time we had been evangelizing, giving away food, and housing homeless men for two years. Our ministry at the restaurant was keeping us busier than ever, and I was being asked to speak more and more. Many of these invitations were from Christian groups in other states. As I began to travel more, Jeanne found it increasingly difficult to manage the restaurant by herself.

One day when I returned from a trip, we talked about this problem. I knew that I had to make a choice. If the Lord was calling me to preach, I would have to close the restaurant. I found it impossible to choose between the two. So, I decided to leave it up to the Lord.

"Jeanne," I said, "next weekend I'll be out of town. You operate the restaurant as usual. If no one shows up on Sunday, we'll shut her down."

Normally Sunday was our busiest day of the week. But on that particular Sunday a huge storm moved in from the Gulf of Mexico. It rained fourteen inches in Pensacola and everything was flooded. It was impossible to drive or even to walk outdoors, so no one came to the restaurant.

When I heard the news I called Jeanne. "When you leave tonight," I told her, "lock the place tight. We're closing."

That decision allowed us to follow the Lord even more closely. It was a great opportunity to walk in faith every day, and the Lord came through. We didn't starve. We didn't even suffer. In fact, in many ways we grew and prospered. Jeanne and I grew closer together every day, and we spent more time with our children because we no longer were pressured by the demands of the restaurant. We also had more time to pray, to study the scriptures, and to pray with people in hospitals and nursing homes.

After I spoke at a few Catholic prayer meetings in northern Florida, other invitations began to come in. I spoke at a number of meetings of the Full Gospel Businessmen's Fellowship and at many Protestant churches.

The more I spoke, the more the little group God had gathered together in Pensacola began to realize that a ministry was in the making. Eventually, I was invited to speak in some Catholic churches and the ministry blossomed. We developed a five-day school of evangelization and were asked to present it in several parishes. Invitations soon arrived from other parts of the country and from Canada. We never sought invitations. The Lord had taught us to walk by faith, relying on him for everything, and he provided everything. The message we presented in the school of evangelization we learned from our experiences with the Lord and from prayer. And the money to support the ministry came from the people who attended the school and responded to the grace they received. It was the beginning of a glorious faith ministry!

When this ministry first began we didn't realize that it would grow beyond one man sharing his testimony at prayer meetings and church services. We were surprised when it did, and we were very thankful for the support of Bishop Gracida and the wisdom of Father Smith to guide us.

After a time it became clear what God's intention for this ministry was: a travelling ministry which called Catholics to respond to the direction given them by the bishops at the Second Vatican Council. The bishops had said to become evangelizers, and we were to help teach Catholics how to do it.

Before long I realized I would be spending a lot of time on the road, or, rather, I would be spending a lot of time in airplanes and at airports. So I decided to study for a pilot's license and ask the Lord for an airplane. It would make travelling much easier.

A few weeks later I offered a businessman a deal. I wanted to trade my restaurant and office building for twenty-seven acres of land and a small airplane. He agreed, and we exchanged titles to the property. About three months later there was a fire in the restaurant and the building burned to the ground. A portion of the office building was also damaged.

The man was enraged. He had failed to purchase insurance on the buildings and he lost a great deal. In addition, the week of the fire his wife told him she was leaving him. What a mess! He was so angry that he drove to the airport and stole the airplane he had traded and took it to his own hangar.

I was furious when I found out. How dare he steal that airplane? Didn't he know it was a crime? Didn't he know I needed it to do the Lord's work?

I called him and demanded that he return the plane within one hour. If he didn't I was going to the sheriff's office and file a complaint.

He hung up without a word.

An hour went by and no airplane. So I got into a car and began driving towards the sheriff's office. While I was on the way, I began to pray in tongues. Father Smith had recommended the practice to me.

While I was praying the Lord spoke to me.

"Whose airplane is it?" I heard him ask me.

"It's yours, Lord," I replied.

"Then don't worry about it. I don't want you putting anybody in jail for taking what belongs to me."

I turned the car around and returned to the airport and picked up Jeanne. We drove to my speaking engagement in Alabama. While we were driving she read the Gospel of Luke to me. She began at chapter one. Nothing seemed significant to me until she read this verse:

> To you who hear me, I say: Love your enemies, do good to those who hate you, bless those who curse you and pray for those who maltreat you. When someone slaps you on one cheek, turn and give him the other; when someone takes your coat, let him have your shirt as well. Give to all who ask you. When a man takes what is yours, do not demand it back. (Lk 6:27-30)

Verse 30, "When a man takes what is yours, do not demand it back," leapt out at me. I knew what I had to do. The Lord did not want me to file charges against the man. He wanted me to let him have the airplane.

I called the man and asked him to forgive me for threatening him. I also told him I would not file charges or threaten him again. He demanded that I return the deed to the twenty-seven acres. My mind returned to the gospel verse, "Give to all who ask you" (Lk 6:30). I had no choice but to return the land to him, even though I knew I would receive nothing in return, not even my own burned-down restaurant building. So I signed over the deed and mailed it back to him.

Three weeks after my airplane was stolen I spoke to several prayer groups in Houston, Texas. One evening, a man I didn't know came to a house where a prayer meeting was being held. He had come not to pray but to borrow something from the homeowner. He listened to me preach and stayed after to talk with me.

I had spoken during the prayer meeting about what I had learned from God's word about not demanding that a robber return something stolen from a Christian.

"Are you serious?" the man asked me. "You're not going to get your airplane back?"

"That's right," I said.

"Well," he replied, "I have five airplanes."

"Brother," I said, "I have need of one."

"Let's go to the airport tomorrow and you can pick one out," he said.

So we did. Later he told me that he was overcome with emotion when he saw me fly off with one of his planes. I had picked the smallest one. But without realizing it, I had chosen his favorite plane. I also found that the plane was worth three times as much as the one that had been stolen from me.

I flew that plane back and forth across North America for two years, travelling from parish to parish. After two years, I had it refurbished inside and out and had a new motor put in it. Then, I returned it to the businessman in Houston. The next week I was in Vermont, where another man gave me an even larger plane. I flew that one for eight months. Then a man in California gave me a twin-engine Aerostar, an excellent airplane, which I flew until 1985.

I believe that all those airplanes, and all the donations of money and supplies which have sustained Good News Ministries from that day on, came our way because we obeyed the Lord. Our ministry is a faith ministry. We have no budgets, no fund-raising efforts, no plans or programs. We accept invitations to preach whenever we can, and we rely on the Lord to give us what we need to minister.

We don't sell anything, either. When I read the gospels, I found out that Jesus never sold anything, so neither do I. In the last six years Good News Ministries has given away tens of thousands of copies of the Vatican Council's Decree on the Apostolate of Lay People and an equal number of sets of audio tapes from our school of evangelization. During the week-long school, we explain our needs and ask the people to make a donation if they feel so moved. From time to time we also mention special needs like TV equipment or repairs on the airplane. That is all the fund-raising we do. We allow the Holy Spirit to move in people's hearts, and we have never been disappointed. God has supplied every need because we have followed him in faith.

We also have a tape ministry, run by a brother and sister named Lenny and Irene Brunelle. Every week Lenny ships about $1,000 worth of tapes and books. We have never charged a penny for these materials.

Lenny and Irene joined our ministry during an evangelism seminar in Burlington, Vermont. He is one of several people whom the Lord has prompted during the seminars to become involved in our ministry. What attracts them? I believe it is the message rather than the ministry itself.

What is the message? We share what God has shown us in our walk with him. We present our testimonies and speak about walking in faith, about patience and love, about the lay person's role in the church, and about the gifts of the Holy Spirit. Everyone who attends the seminars or listens to the tapes is invited to give his or her life to Jesus Christ and to follow him as an active lay man or woman in the church.

Our goals are very simple. We want to open the doors of spiritual experience to Catholics, and we expect them to walk through those doors and encounter the Lord. By the end of the school, most participants have committed their lives to Jesus, been baptized in the Holy Spirit, and received the gift of tongues. If they then commit themselves to prayer and to reading the scriptures and the decree on the laity, the Lord will show them what to do next.

Everyone who follows this simple program sooner or later finds God prompting them to tell others what he has done for them. This is evangelization—spreading the good news of the love and mercy of Jesus. The teachings of scripture and the church make it very clear: we must evangelize. We must tell others about the Lord.

Often, however, we are afraid to speak about the Lord. Fear is the biggest obstacle most Christians face in sharing the good news, and the remedy for fear is to identify it and get rid of it. The Bible gives us several keys to identifying fear. The primary one I have found is in the third chapter of Genesis.

Genesis tells us that the serpent, "the most cunning of all the animals that the Lord God had made," played on Eve's pride to persuade her to disobey God. The serpent told her that if she ate of the fruit that God had forbidden, she would be like a god herself, able to distinguish good from evil. Eve resisted the tempter for a while, but in the end she gave in to him. Adam did likewise, and the sin of the first humans has been wreaking havoc on the human race ever since.

According to the Bible, the first ill effect of the sin of Adam and Eve was fear:

> When they [Adam and Eve] heard the sound of the Lord God moving about in the garden at the breezy time of the day, the man and his wife hid themselves from the Lord

> God among the trees of the garden. The Lord God then called to the man and asked him, "Where are you?" He answered, "I heard you in the garden; but I was afraid, because I was naked, so I hid myself." (Gn 3:8-9)

Adam was afraid because he knew that what he had done had separated him from God. He knew there was no hope for him. He knew that now he would live under the rule and power of Satan and that he would have to die. As he realized all these things, fear crept over him. That fear has reigned over all the earth ever since.

As a result of sin, human beings became afraid of God, afraid of the one who had given them life and love, the one who had walked with them "in the breezy part of the day," showing them great affection. It was all gone in an instant because of sin. Adam and Eve got what the serpent told them they would get—knowledge of good and evil, knowledge that would make them like gods. But they also received a curse that has been handed down from generation to generation. The first manifestation of that curse—fear—is still with us, keeping us from doing the things God wants us to do.

Fortunately, God was not content to leave things in this state. As the Bible says:

> If by the offense of the one man [Adam] all died, much more did the grace of God and the gracious gift of the one man, Jesus Christ, abound for all. . . . If death began its reign through one man because of his offense, much more shall those who receive the overflowing grace and gift of justice live and reign through the one man, Jesus Christ. To sum up, then: just as a single offense brought condemnation to all men, a single righteous act brought all men acquittal and life." (Rom 6:15-18)

We don't need to be afraid anymore. The sin of Adam and Eve brought fear into the world, but the victory of Jesus—his death and resurrection—eliminated the root cause of fear. Jesus defeated Satan, the father of fear, and vanquished fear and death forever. The Bible tells us that in Christ there is no death. We are going to live forever. In Christ we have the joy of knowing that we are on the way to eternal glory, that we will wear crowns and live with Jesus forever. There is nothing to fear.

Yet we are still afraid. We don't realize the power that Jesus has to cast fear out of our lives. I was once leading a meeting in California when I noticed a crippled woman walk in, hunched over a cane. It took her about fifteen minutes to get into a chair, and then she sat there shaking. My subject that night was fear, and when I finished speaking the woman came up to me and said, "I am scared to death."

"I can tell," I answered. "You're about ready to die, aren't you, sister?"

She nodded her head and said, "I am."

"Well," I said, "we're going to get rid of that fear."

Then I prayed: "Satan, in the name of Jesus Christ, who defeated you and cast out your fear, I command you to loose your hold of fear on my sister. Get away from her right now."

Immediately she threw down her cane, straightened up, and walked out the door, exclaiming, "Hallelujah!"

Fear had crippled her inside and out. But when she heard the truth about Jesus, she believed and allowed him to drive fear out of her life. Many of us are crippled internally, if not externally, by fear. We are afraid of the dark. We are afraid of criminals. We are afraid of losing our money. We are afraid of failure. Worst of all, we may be afraid that others will ridicule us if we live like Christians, so we hide our Christian faith under a bushel basket.

We don't have to live with those fears! Jesus has poured so much love into our lives through his life, his teaching, his death, and his resurrection, that he has eliminated the need to be afraid. He has loved us with a perfect, everlasting love, and "perfect love casts out all fear" (1 Jn 4:18).

In the very first chapter of the last book of the Bible, the book of Revelation, the visionary John saw the Lord Jesus Christ, the great and mighty King, reigning in the heavens. John was afraid and "fell down at his feet as though dead."

Jesus touched him and said: "There is nothing to fear. I am the First and the Last and the One who lives. Once I was dead and now I live—forever and ever. I hold the keys of death and the nether world" (Rv 1:17-18).

Jesus says the same thing to us today: "There's nothing to fear. I have won the victory. I hold the keys of death. If you belong to me, nothing can touch you unless I allow it. I am the one who lives forever and ever. Put your trust in me. You don't need to fear."

Many of us have been tormented by fear all our lives because of a spirit of fear sent by the devil, which causes us to be caught and bound by fear. Satan wants fear to grip people's hearts so they will die without having lived for the kingdom of God. He is frequently successful. Many people die when fear grips their hearts. They begin to fear old age or losing their job or losing their possessions. Then their hands freeze, their minds stop functioning, they panic, and they die.

Several times when piloting an airplane, I have encountered mechanical failures and sudden violent weather. If I had not known that Jesus' love has cast fear out of my life, I would have panicked. I would have allowed fear to grip my heart. Fear would have frozen my mind and kept my hands from doing what they needed to do to get me through the situation.

I once lived in a state of fear. Now I live in a state of faith. Jesus replaced fear with faith. Satan no longer has a hold on me because I am a child of God. Jesus has conquered him in my life.

This is one of the most important results of surrendering our lives to Jesus. When we accept the Lord and begin to live in a state of faith, we no longer need to be afraid. All we need to do is turn to the Lord, identify our fears, and cast them out in the name of Jesus. Are you afraid of failure? Cast it out. There are no failures in the kingdom of God, only saints redeemed by Jesus Christ. Are you afraid of losing your money? Cast out that fear. You don't need money to be happy—you need Jesus. Once you have Jesus in your life, you'll never be in want of anything. He'll take care of you. Are you timid, afraid of facing life head on? Cast it out. Jesus wants you to be a bold Christian, filled with joy and fervor for sharing the good news of salvation with others.

When you identify your fears as best you can, get down on your knees and pray, "Go away, Satan, and take your spirit of fear with you. I am a child of God, redeemed by the blood of Jesus. You no longer have any hold over me."

Then let Jesus fill you with faith, hope, and love. You will be free from fear. You may sometimes be tempted to let fear creep back into your life, but when this happens, rebuke it. Tell Satan that, like John in the book of Revelation, you have seen the Lord and he told you "there is nothing to fear." Satan can't tolerate that kind of talk. He'll be gone as quickly as if you had jabbed him with a hot poker.

When we are free of fear, we can do what God wants us to do. We can live in his love, and we can spread that love around by evangelizing. That's why we are on this earth in the first place, and when we get busy with the job not only does fear stay far away, but so do a lot of other problems. If we are busy evangelizing, we won't have time for greed, envy, laziness, or lust. We'll be too busy loving to have time for sinning. Does this sound simplistic? Too good to be true? Give it a try!

When we are freed from fear, we can fulfill our role as evangelizers and sanctifiers. But to do this effectively and according to the spirit of the gospel of Jesus Christ, we also must learn to love. Shortly after I committed my life to Jesus, I had to learn how to forgive and love a man who had committed one of the most grisly sins anyone can commit.

SEVEN

Loving People into the Kingdom

"I'VE COME TO ASK YOUR FORGIVENESS FOR HATING YOU."

Forcing those words out of my mouth was one of the most difficult things I have ever done. They were addressed to my next-door neighbor, whom I had hated with a passion for eight years. I would lie awake at night, thinking about ways I could kill him. I fantasized about car bombs, about hiring a hit man from New York, about setting his house on fire in the middle of the night.

The hatred I felt towards this man had contributed to the drinking problem I had developed. The consuming desire for revenge and the drinking resulted in high blood pressure, a hernia, and several other problems. My health was a wreck.

Why did I hate him so much? He had repeatedly molested my son and daughter. My son was eight and my daughter six when this all started, and it was two years before we discovered it. When we finally did, it was just too much for me. I thought about my little children being stripped of their dignity, and I couldn't stand it, and the hatred began to grow.

I was completely serious about killing the man, but I never followed through because I didn't want to go to jail. Only the fear of a prison term kept me from murder. When I finally gave up the idea of killing him, I built an eight-foot fence between his house and ours so that I at least wouldn't have to see him. The sight of him made me sick to my stomach.

Forgive him? How could I? He was sick, but that didn't move me. He had committed an offense against something very precious to me, and I could only react with hatred.

After I committed my life to Jesus, Father Jim Smith began to teach me about forgiveness and unconditional love. He showed me the scriptures that commanded me to love everyone—people who had hurt me as well as people who had been good to me.

"You mean I have to love the man who molested my children?" I asked in disbelief. "Why, he's a horrible human being. He hurt two of God's little children. It's hard enough to think about forgiving him. The idea of loving him makes me ill."

Father Smith was a good and gentle man, but he kept confronting me with the truth:

> If you forgive the faults of others, your heavenly Father will forgive you yours. If you do not forgive others, neither will your Father forgive you." (Mt 6:14-15)

> To you who hear me, I say: Love your enemies, do good to those who hate you, bless those who curse you and pray for those who maltreat you. . . . Then you will rightly be called sons of the Most High, since he himself is good to the ungrateful and the wicked." (Lk 6:27, 35)

As I prayed about those scriptures and recalled how much the Lord had forgiven me, I realized that I had no choice but to forgive *everyone* who had offended me. I had already forgiven my wife. That was relatively easy because when I experienced the love of the Lord Jesus in my life, I came to love her. But that monster next door was another question.

If it had not been for the scriptures, I could not have done it. But they are crystal clear: forgive *all* who have offended you; love them because God loves them. When I accepted those truths, I realized that if God had ever stopped loving me during my years of sin, I would have died and gone to hell. If Jeanne had held grievances against me, it would have been difficult for me to surrender my life to Jesus. When she forgave me, she released me from the many sins I'd committed against her. Scripture says:

> I assure you, whatever you declare bound on earth shall be held bound in heaven, and whatever you declare loosed on earth shall be held loosed in heaven. (Mt 18:18)

Many Catholics think that this passage refers only to the authority of the clergy to forgive sins in Jesus' name in the sacrament of reconciliation. But the authority of the clergy is actually based more on another passage, Matthew 16:19, where Jesus confers the power to bind and loose on Peter and his successors, the bishops and priests of the church. In Matthew 18, Jesus tells all his disciples that they have the power to bind and loose the sins of others. We can interfere with the flow of God's forgiveness into another person's life if we don't forgive them. But must I forgive someone like my neighbor or Adolf Hitler? Jesus says, "If you do not forgive others, neither will your Father forgive you" (Mt 6:15).

There's an expression that goes like this: "I'll see that guy in hell before I'll forgive him." Well, that's exactly where you'll see him if you don't forgive him because you'll both be there.

Forgiveness and love are extremely important for Christians. When I forgave my neighbor, God did some extraordinary things. About three months later my wife was shopping in a supermarket and the man approached her. He pulled a copy of the New Testament out of his pocket and told Jeanne that he had given his life to Jesus. He had been reconciled with the Catholic Church, which he had abandoned years before, and had confessed his sins. He had received God's forgiveness and wanted to thank us for forgiving him.

Three weeks later the man died. Where would his soul be today if I had not forgiven him? I thank God for Father Smith who taught me this truth while there was time. Even though I did not have the opportunity to explicitly tell him about the Lord, my act of forgiveness prompted him to think about his own need for forgiveness.

When God tells us to be merciful and to love unconditionally, he means that we are to love *everyone*. Whether they are attractive or unattractive, good or wicked, we must love them because our Father in heaven loves them, and Jesus commands us to be perfect just as our heavenly Father is perfect (see Mt 5:48).

Most people today, even Christians, do not understand what love is. Many of us have never seriously considered what the scriptures say about love. For example:

> The man without love has known nothing of God, for God is love. (1 Jn 4:7)

> Love, then, consists in this: not that we have loved God but that he has loved us and has sent his Son as an offering for our sins.... Beloved, if God has loved us so, we must have the same love for one another. No one has ever seen God. Yet if we love one another God dwells in us and his love is brought to perfection in us.... If anyone says, "My love is fixed on God," yet hates his brother, he is a liar. One who has not love for the brother he has seen cannot love the God he has not seen. The commandment we have from him is this: whoever loves God must also love his brother.
> (1 Jn 4:10-12, 20-21)

John says that if you don't love the brother you can see, you don't love the God you cannot see. If you don't love your brother, he says, but say you love God, you're a liar. He also says:

> The man who does not love is among the living dead. Anyone who hates his brother is a murderer, and you know that eternal life abides in no murderer's heart.
>
> (1 Jn 3:14-15)

When Father Smith was teaching me about love, the verse about the man who hates being a murderer drove the point home to me. "What's a worse sin," he asked, "rape or murder?"

"Murder," I answered.

"You don't want God to look upon you as a murderer, do you?"

No, I didn't. No one does. So we must love, unconditionally, as does the Lord, "for his sun rises on the bad and the good, he rains on the just and the unjust" (Mt 5:45). I had to stop murdering my neighbor in my heart, and then I had to start loving him unconditionally so that he could give his life to Jesus and embrace the kingdom of God. It was tremendously difficult, but it reaped everlasting rewards. I'm convinced that my neighbor is now in heaven.

The message of love is at the heart of our Christian faith. We love others because God first loved us, and to be true to his love, we must love everyone. Some Christians interpret the scripture passages about love as referring only to loving other Christians. After all, John uses the word "brother." Yet who is our brother? The Nicene Creed, the public expression of the content of our faith, says, "I believe in one God, the Father, the Almighty, maker of heaven and earth, of all that is seen and unseen."

If God is the Maker of all, then all human beings belong to

him. Even those who have not accepted his love? Yes. Scripture clearly shows that God loves all his creatures. This is our call also. When a lawyer confronted Jesus with the question, "Who is my neighbor?" Jesus told him the parable of the Good Samaritan (see Lk 10:25-35):

> "Which of these three," Jesus asked him after finishing the parable, "was neighbor to the man who fell in with the robbers?" The answer came, "The one who treated him with compassion." Jesus said to him, "Then go and do the same." (Lk 10:36-37)

This passage also teaches us what love is. Love is caring for another. Love is having compassion for another. Love is serving the needs of another. In his famous teaching on using the gifts of the Holy Spirit in love, the Apostle Paul tells us:

> Love is patient; love is kind. Love is not jealous, it does not put on airs, it is not snobbish. Love is never rude, it is not self-seeking, it is not prone to anger; neither does it brood over injuries. Love does not rejoice in what is wrong, but rejoices in the truth. There is no limit to love's forbearance, to its trust, its hope, its power to endure. . . . There are in the end three things that last: faith, hope and love, and the greatest of these is love. (1 Cor 13:4-7, 13)

Christians are to love. It is our first and highest calling. Everything we do should flow from the love of God which fills our hearts. If we do not love, we are not doing God's work.

Learning about love from the teachings of Scripture and the church set me free internally. My relationships with my children, which had been very poor because of my years of drinking and chasing the dollar, were gradually healed. I learned to share the love of God not only with them, but with everyone I met. And I learned that the only way to evangelize is to love people into the kingdom of God.

When, by the grace of God, I decided to love the neighbor who had molested my children, I was able to evangelize him. I didn't preach at him or berate him for his sin. I forgave him. I loved him. The result was repentance. That's real evangelism. That's loving people into the kingdom of God.

When I realized the power of love, I knew that I could also love my children into the kingdom of God. They had all rejected God and the church, primarily because of my bad example. They had seen me go to church, yet fail to live the faith, so they tuned church out. They rebelled against authority, which they had also learned from me. I needed to live what I preached in order to undo the effects of many years of bad example. I had to be patient, control my anger, and put the concerns of others ahead of my own. For me, it meant learning a completely new way of relating, and it took years. I had to put off the mind of Charlie Osburn and put on the "mind of Christ" (1 Cor 2:16). The mind of Christ is love, self-sacrificing love, for others (see Phil 2:5-8).

One day the sheriff's department called me. One of my sons was in jail. He had been caught drag racing on a city street. He had never been in trouble with the law before, and I could have let him sit in jail for a while to "learn his lesson." But I don't think that would have displayed the unconditional love which God calls us to show. So I dropped what I was doing and drove over to the jail. When I was brought to his cell I said, "Son, don't you know that I love you?" I was concerned that he had perceived a lack of love in me and was getting into trouble in order to strike back.

"Yes, Daddy," he answered. "I know you love me."

"Let's go home, then."

I decided to love my son, to stand by him, no matter what he had done. Jeanne and I had to stand by him and patiently pray for him for six troubled years. During those years he became increasingly rebellious. I could have tried to change him. I could have preached at him, yelled at him, or thrown him out of the house. Many people would have advocated doing these things, calling it "tough love." But I decided not to. I wanted to follow what the gospel teaches about love.

During those six years of patiently loving our son and praying for him, Jeanne and I were tried many times. He was a rebellious young man, a hurting young man. We knew that only when his heart was filled with the love of Jesus would he be healed of those hurts. We longed with all our hearts for him to commit his life to the Lord, but we knew that he had to decide that for himself. No one can force a decision for Jesus Christ on someone else. All we could do was continually show him the love of Jesus, doing our best to love him into the kingdom of God.

Finally, when he was twenty-three years old, he had had enough of the life he was living and invited Jesus into his life. A few weeks later, on Father's Day, the five Osburn children gave me a new Bible, each writing a message in it. This son, for whom we had so patiently prayed, had written: "I love you, Dad, for loving me into the kingdom of God."

I was overwhelmed at the goodness of God. He never allows loving actions to go unrewarded. The Bible is full of promises for those who trust in God and obey him. And what better reward is there for Christian parents than to see their children give their lives to Jesus?

One by one, the Osburn children came to the Lord. Each had obstacles to overcome, walls to tear down, grief to suffer. But Jeanne and I had learned the lesson about love, and the Lord was faithful. We were patient and kind with our children. We never took offense at the things they did or said. We stood by them and helped them. Whenever they needed anything, we gave it to them. And that, according to God's holy word, is what love is all about.

Today, in the schools of evangelization, I teach people that the best way, the only way, to evangelize is to love people into the kingdom. When we are patient, kind, gentle, and self-controlled, we manifest the love of Jesus. And when others see the love of Jesus in us, they much more easily believe what we say.

How do Christians evangelize?

First, by living the word. By giving a good example. You can't show Jesus to others if you are not living his word. We must be as sincere a witness to Christ in the way we live as we are in our preaching.

The Vatican Council's Decree on the Apostolate of Lay People says this:

> The true apostle is on the lookout for occasions of announcing Christ by word, either to unbelievers to draw them toward the faith, or to the faithful to instruct them, strengthen them, incite them to a more fervent life; for Christ's love urges us on.

We are surrounded with "occasions of announcing Christ by word." The words we speak to those we live with—our spouses, children, roommates—are such occasions. A warm, loving "hello and God bless you today" is the best way I know to greet someone in the morning. It announces Christ, if it is sincere and loving. If you're not sincere, you should probably keep quiet.

We can also announce Christ by sharing our testimonies and telling others what the Lord has done for us. I was trying to sleep in one Saturday morning, since I had gotten home very late the night before. At about nine o'clock my wife began singing very loudly in the kitchen in tongues. I grew irritated because she knew I wanted to sleep. So I tramped down the hall and confronted her.

"What on earth is going on?" I asked.

"The washing machine is broken," she replied.

"Why does that make you happy?"

"Because I get to tell the repairman about the love of Jesus."

Does this sound silly? It's not. Jeanne was overjoyed to

have the repairman come, because she could tell him about Jesus. And she did. The love of Christ urged her on.

Every time we encounter someone, whether it's in our home or theirs, in a store or on a bus, we have an opportunity to "announce Christ by word." It can be a very short word, such as "Hello, God bless you." Or, if the opportunity presents itself, it can be a full-blown witness about Jesus. The important thing is that we be open to the Holy Spirit and allow him to direct us.

People in need are often the most open to hearing about Christ. Be on the lookout for people who are distressed, hungry, or sick, and ask them, "May I pray with you about this problem?" "Can I buy you a meal?" "May I cook or clean for your family while you're in the hospital?" And in the midst of that prayer ministry, or that meal, or that work of mercy, ask the most important question: "May I tell you about the love of Jesus?" "May I tell you about what Jesus Christ has done for me?" "May I tell you what he can do for you and your family?"

Evangelization is not a technique, a plan, or a program. It is a willingness to live the life of Christ and a decision to do so. When you are open, loving, patient, and kind in whatever you do, living the love of Jesus as well as speaking about it, you are an evangelist. When you practice what you preach, when you live life in Christ to its fullest, then you can't help but proclaim Jesus in whatever you do and say.

I now find it very difficult to talk about the weather or the government. Topics like these bore me. They change. They usually disappoint us. But Jesus is exciting, and Jesus never changes. He never disappoints. Now that I base everything I do on him, on his word, and on his love, life is thrilling, challenging, rewarding.

Certainly I have disappointments. I have aches and pains. People sometimes ridicule me and even actively oppose my work. But Jesus said these things would happen to those who follow him. I don't let them worry me. I just do what the

Lord tells me to do and let the chips fall where they may. Christians are supposed to live this way.

I had preached this message of love and patience, and their impact on evangelization, in Catholic churches across the United States, Canada, and the Philippines. And as the number of people affected by it grew, so did my desire to share it on television.

The beginning of our television ministry dates back to June 23, 1984, my fifty-first birthday, when I flew my airplane from San Francisco to Pensacola to spend a few days at home. It is a long flight, and by the time I got home I was exhausted. While I was sleeping that night I dreamed that I was in a house full of tables of beautiful food. Every room I entered was full of food, and I went from table to table, eating.

Suddenly, two men came up, handcuffed me, and took me to a car, not saying a word. They drove to an abandoned field with a high iron-bar fence. I knew it was a jail. When I asked why I was being jailed, the two men refused to answer. They just got back into the car and drove away.

Well, this imprisonment agitated me, and I asked the Lord, "What's going on here?"

"You're in jail," he answered.

"I can see that, Lord. What I want to know is why."

No answer.

"Well, then, what do I have to do to get out?"

"Fast and pray."

"For how long?"

"Fourteen days."

"Fourteen days! I can't go fourteen days without food."

"Then stay in jail."

I woke up in a sweat and told Jeanne about the dream. "I have to fast for fourteen days—no food at all. Nothing but water."

Jeanne supported me, of course. I couldn't have made it without her.

On the fourth day of the fast I went to our office to work. I was feeling very weak by then, and when I got there all I could do was lie down on the sofa. My son Brian was in the office. He wore his hair long and had a beard and strange-looking clothes. He'd been working with us for about two years but had not committed his life to the Lord. Nevertheless, I treated him exactly the way I preach. I was patient, kind, and loving with him. For eight years, I had been loving my son into the kingdom of God.

I quickly finished the business I had come there to do and then I left. After I was gone Brian looked over at his mother and said, "Mom, what's wrong with Dad?"

"I'm really supposed to keep this quiet," she said. "But I can tell you, Brian. Your father is on a fourteen-day fast."

"Dad can't fast for fourteen days," he said.

"I know that, you know that, and Dad knows that, but God apparently knows something different, because he ordered it."

That conversation really affected Brian. I wasn't there, of course, but Jeanne says that a few minutes after her conversation with him Brian got up out of his chair without saying a word. An hour later he came back clean shaven and his hair cut short. "I've just committed my life to Jesus," he said. "I'm giving you notice that I'm here to serve the Lord Jesus Christ."

That was the first miracle of the fast. The second miracle occurred on the ninth day. I was in the office when an editor from *New Covenant* magazine called. *New Covenant* is a magazine devoted to spiritual renewal in the Catholic Church. The editor told Brian that they wanted to feature an article about me and put my picture on the cover.

After that article was published in September, we received telephone calls and letters from all over the world. And that was the month our television ministry began to move from dream to reality.

I still don't fully understand why God wanted me to fast those fourteen days, but I know the fruit of it. My son committed his life to Jesus and was released from his own kind of prison. And our ministry began to take on international significance. There has been a tremendous amount of fruit in my own life and in the ministry since that fast. But the big story is the television ministry.

EIGHT

Broadcast Ministry

IT WAS IN 1981 that my preaching ministry began to develop. I didn't fully understand the gift that God had given me, but I knew that the Holy Spirit had given me wisdom which he wanted me to place at the service of the church.

This wisdom concerned the authority and tradition of the Catholic Church and how Scripture can be understood in the light of them. As I began to understand the richness of the church's traditions and the great power that God has placed in the church's authority, I also began to understand Scripture more fully. And as I proclaimed these truths as a layman, people began suggesting that I preach on television.

Although I liked the idea, I also knew that television time is extremely expensive. So, whenever I heard that comment, I would reply, "I'll go on television when you learn how to support me."

For four years I strongly desired to tell the millions who watch Christian television about unconditional love and lay people ministering in faith. But it was only a desire. I had no idea how to make that desire a reality. However, I believed that God wanted to make it a reality. And since I knew that he can do anything, I didn't worry about it or even look for someone to put me on the air.

The Lord has taught me to look at desires and hopes with eyes of faith. When we look at things the way we know God wants them to be, rather than the way they are, then our hope is based in reality. I placed the whole area of television into God's hands. That doesn't mean I didn't speak about it to people. I surely did. But I didn't worry. I knew that God had a plan. I just needed to patiently walk in faith until he made his plan known to me.

God began to reveal the first phase of his plan in January of 1983. I was preaching that month in Calexico, California. One day, David du Plessis, the renowned Pentecostal leader, called to tell me that a friend of his from Denver, Colorado, had asked him to recommend a Catholic evangelist who could minister to his people. This friend was Charles Blair, the pastor of Calvary Temple, a large Pentecostal congregation which counted among its members hundreds of former Catholics.

When I arrived at Calvary Temple, I noticed that it was full of television equipment for the church's own productions, so I told Pastor Blair about the week-long school of evangelism that I had been conducting in Catholic churches. Would he be interested in holding one in his church and taping it for possible television broadcast?

"That's a great idea," Pastor Blair said. "It would teach our congregation how our Catholic brothers and sisters win souls for Jesus. Let's do it!"

"Okay," I said. "Now all we need is the permission of your bishop."

"I don't have a bishop," he said. "This is a non-denominational church."

"Yes, you do," I replied. "He's down the street at the Catholic Pastoral Center. His name is Archbishop James V. Casey. Why don't you go down and ask him if I can come into your church and present my seminar on Catholic evangelism?"

Pastor Blair did that and Archbishop Casey gave us permission. We decided to conduct the school during February of the following year, and agreed to tape all the sessions. Because I suspected that this was to be the beginning of my television ministry, I left Denver rejoicing in the plan that the Lord had begun to reveal.

One year later I was in southern California, preparing for the seminar at Calvary Temple. I had prayed all year for this new television ministry. Pastor Blair had agreed to videotape the seminar, but when the teaching was over, he would hand me the seminar tapes and I would be on my own. So I had been asking the Lord to send someone who could produce the television ministry.

Shortly before leaving for Denver, my wife and I were at a restaurant in San Diego with another couple, Jack and Elizabeth Hendricks, who were coming with us. We were talking enthusiastically about the wonderful things the Lord was doing in our ministry, and especially about the additional means we saw in television for us to bring his message to the whole world.

While we were talking, a young man approached us and said, "My name is Bruce Cooley. It is really exciting to hear someone talk about Jesus."

"Yes," I replied. "Everyone at this table is really excited about Jesus."

Bruce gave me his business card and told me to contact him if I ever needed his services. Then he left, without saying what those services were. Since I was in the middle of lunch, I put the card in my pocket without reading it. A few minutes later I was told I was wanted on the telephone.

When I picked up the phone, the voice on the other end said, "This is Bruce Cooley. I came to your table a little while ago and left you my card, but I really didn't do what I was supposed to do. I was supposed to offer you my services. Is there anything I can do to help you?"

"Brother," I answered, "what do you do?"

"I'm an audio-video technician. I put together television programs for businesses."

So I told him about the plans we had for videotaping in

Denver. "I really need someone to take charge of that material once it's on tape."

"I'd like to do that for you," Bruce said.

We met together and decided that God wanted Bruce to be part of Good News Ministries. The ministry purchased a commercial-grade television camera and a portable videotape pack. Bruce then followed us around, taking shots of everything we did. He would later edit them and use them to create introductory and closing segments for our program.

The Denver taping did not go well at all, and we have never used the tapes. But we now had Bruce and all his expertise. Soon we purchased additional television equipment in order to do our own taping.

One evening, while I was conducting a school of evangelization in Lethbridge, Alberta, Canada, I mentioned that we hoped someday to televise the school. The only obstacle to this dream becoming a reality, I said, was the cost. The next evening a woman came up to me after my presentation and handed me a cashier's check for $27,000 to be used for the television ministry.

We used the money to purchase video recorders and other equipment. At this point we had about half of what was needed to produce quality programs.

Three weeks later I was at the Pensacola airport when a man charged up to me and asked about my airplane. The plane had a big dove painted on the tail and the words "Jesus is Lord" over the windows. We also had painted our "Good News Ministries" logo, as well as the words "Holy Ghost Airlines" on the plane. The man wanted to know what church I belonged to. He was flabbergasted when I told him I was Catholic.

"So am I," he said, "but I've never heard of anything like this."

"Well," I said, "get used to it because this is the future of the church."

I told him that Catholics were discovering what it meant to give their lives to Jesus. It is only a matter of time, I said, before Catholics by the millions would begin reaching out to the whole world with the excitement of the Holy Spirit.

He then told me that his two daughters had recently left the Catholic Church and joined a church whose pentecostal leader preached against Catholicism. This man's family was in the middle of a serious spiritual crisis.

I didn't have time to talk with him because I was scheduled to fly out of Pensacola just a few minutes later, so I gave him a set of evangelization tapes.

"Listen to these," I said, "and then give them to your daughters. I believe it will help you solve your problem."

Later he called me and told me he had listened to the entire set in the following twenty-four hours.

"I've never heard anything like this before," he said. "I've been a Catholic all my life, studied for years under Jesuits, and attended all kinds of retreats and seminars. But no one has ever explained the faith to me like this. I have really been blessed."

In one of those tapes I had mentioned that we needed $16,000 for additional television equipment. This man was so moved by the tapes that he wanted to help our ministry. "Where can I send the check?" he asked. A few days later his check for $16,000 arrived in the mail. We used it to purchase the additional equipment we needed.

The following week we gave the evangelization seminar in Phoenix, Arizona, where the Lord deeply touched several people who contributed a total of $21,000.

All during this time Bruce Cooley travelled with me, taping most of my talks. One day he told me that we now had enough equipment and enough raw tape to begin a television program, so I asked him to call someone in the Christian television business and find out how much a weekly program would cost. We had discovered how incredibly expensive television is. We had already spent more than $80,000 on equipment and taping and still hadn't put a single minute of our message on the air.

Bruce called Trinity Broadcasting, a Christian network based in the Los Angeles area. He told a sales representative that we were interested in buying time.

"Who are you?" she asked.

Bruce told her that we were a Catholic evangelistic organization.

"A Catholic evangelist? I've never heard of a Catholic evangelist!"

This woman, who had grown up a Catholic but had joined another church, became intrigued with our ministry and decided to come to Arizona and hear me preach. She brought another Trinity staff member with her, and they stayed for two days, listening to our teaching and talking to us. When they left, they seemed excited about what we were doing, and tentatively offered us a $3,300 per hour time slot.

The thought of spending $3,300 a week for television time, plus the additional cost of equipment, personnel, and so on, would frighten many people. That's a great deal of money. But this ministry is a faith ministry. I didn't waste a single moment worrying because I knew the Lord was leading the way. If he wanted a weekly television program featuring a Catholic lay evangelist, he'd supply the money we needed. So I turned to him and said, "You've given us all this equipment. So please provide the rest of what we need." He did. We received a donation in that amount within a few days.

Two weeks later I was preaching in Mammoth, a small mining town in the mountains of Arizona, when Paul Crouch, the president of Trinity Broadcasting, called and asked to meet with me in California. We scheduled the meeting for December of 1984. I also arranged to have at that meeting three men who had been supporting our ministry: Bill Isbell, past president of the Ramada Inn motel chain; Louis Michot, the man from Louisiana who had given us the $16,000; and Bud Hartigan, an airlines captain. Each of them had encountered the Lord through our ministry, and each was an astute businessman. I wanted them to be at the meeting with Paul Crouch to advise me.

Trinity proposed a contract that did not include the $3,300 charge. Instead, the network wanted to sponsor me and even offered us the use of their studios. Paul Crouch explained all the details, proposing a thirty-minute prime-time slot.

Bud Hartigan listened to this and then spoke up. "Charlie can't even say his name in thirty minutes," he said. "He needs at least an hour."

The program director, who is responsible for scheduling, said, "We don't have an hour available. All we have is thirty minutes."

"We may not have an hour," Crouch said, "but we'll find one. We want your program, and you'll have that hour."

During our meeting Paul said he was very impressed with the Vatican Council's Decree on the Apostolate of Lay People. The network representatives who had attended the seminar had brought several copies of the decree back with them, and Paul had read it. "My own Assemblies of God Church should adopt this document as a guideline for lay ministry," he said.

He was excited about the document, about the spiritual vitality he saw coming from the Catholic community, and about my God-given ability to preach. He wanted some of that vitality on his network.

Paul was also impressed with Catholicism for personal reasons. His eldest son was baptized in the Holy Spirit in a Catholic church, and several people in his organization have close ties with the church. These contacts produced in him an openness towards the Catholic Church and fueled his excitement over our seminar tapes and the council document.

While we were in California discussing our program, Paul asked Jeanne and me to appear as guests on his show, "Praise the Lord." Our appearance generated a great response from viewers, and the greatest excitement was over my being a Catholic. The Protestant viewers just loved to hear a Catholic lay evangelist preach to them about Jesus.

When I thought about what Paul had said and about the response of his viewers to our appearance on his show, I marvelled at how God had used Protestants to sponsor a Catholic evangelist on television. I had been preaching for four years with a mandate from my bishop and was enthusiastically supported by many other Catholic leaders. Yet Catholics had not been able to support our television outreach. We had to turn to a Protestant network.

What do I preach? I explain the documents of Vatican II, the Creed, and other basic Catholic beliefs, and I relate them to our message of faith and to the Scriptures. It is a conservative Catholic message. I preach about submitting to the authority of the church and about loving the church, our spouses, our children, and everyone else with unconditional love.

Almost all of the mail that criticizes our message comes from Catholics and former Catholics. Most of these are people who for some reason left the church and are now angry and bitter. Some people also feel that my theology leaves something to be desired. They consider me a fundamentalist. Yet all I preach is the Creed and the documents of Vatican II. These documents are loaded with references to Scripture. I simply look up the Scripture references and talk about them. It's the bishops of Vatican II who approved the documents. I'm just telling the public what they had to say to the Catholics of our day about our mission in the church and the world.

Because of the great way in which God had provided for us through Trinity Broadcasting, we expected great things from this television ministry. We had been given enough money to purchase almost all the equipment we needed and had now received free time on a nationwide network. However, God wasn't finished. He wanted to provide a way for us to move our equipment around the country.

Not long after our meetings with Trinity, I conducted an evangelization seminar at a parish in the San Diego area. One morning I walked out of the home in which I was staying and saw a bus parked there. I wouldn't have given the bus a second thought except that it was painted in the same colors as my airplane. It was white on top, tan on the bottom, and had an orange and a brown stripe running around it. My airplane has an identical color scheme.

I turned to my host and said, "Bob, your bus is painted the same colors as my airplane. I wonder if the Lord is telling me something about that bus."

"Well," he replied. "I hope not because I plan to convert it into a motor home so my wife and I can travel around the country."

But I couldn't stop looking at the bus. Something was stirring inside me. Bob told me he had bought it from a dealer nearby who had purchased a whole fleet of nineteen-foot Mercedes diesel buses from a mass transit company and was selling them one at a time. I couldn't do anything about it then, but for an entire month that bus was never far from my mind. Then one day I felt that God wanted me to buy one of those buses. A man in the parish I was speaking at gave our ministry $7,300, so I went to the dealer's lot and purchased one.

The dealer serviced the bus and told us it was ready to go. We headed east but the bus wouldn't make it over the mountain. We had to have it towed back to San Diego. I called the dealer and asked him to service it again. If it couldn't make it over that mountain, it would be of no use to us.

I left Bruce to look after the bus and I flew to Yuma, Arizona, to present another school of evangelization. The dealer in California got the bus running again, and Bruce drove it over the mountain and through the desert into Yuma. But when he got to Yuma the engine blew up.

That seemed like the last straw. The bus would never run the way we needed it to, so I told Bruce to sell it to a junkyard. That night, while I was preaching in Yuma, I told the story about the bus.

Afterwards a man came forward and offered to rebuild the engine. I agreed, and he and his associates set to work. They rebuilt the engine, the fuel system, the cooling system—all the running parts. When they were finished, that little bus ran great.

While they were finishing their work, a man named Barry called to say that he had heard me preach on television, had ordered my tapes, and had experienced the Lord very powerfully through them. He had been separated from his wife but after hearing our teaching had been reconciled with her. He was so excited. He also told me that he had a 5,000 watt electric generator.

"The Lord impressed upon me that you needed a generator," he said. "Can you use it?"

I told him about the bus that was being repaired in Yuma. "We are turning the bus into a television studio so that we can produce television programs while we travel."

"Great," he said. "Does it need to be painted?"

"It's in bad shape," I answered. "It's all banged up and really could use a paint job."

"Well, I own a paint and body shop," he said, "and I'd love to straighten it up for you."

Well, Barry and his crew did a fine job on that bus. They took out most of the windows and replaced them with metal panels so we could do television work inside. Then they flushed the bus out, repaired all the dents in the exterior, and painted it. When they were finished it looked magnificent and made a great studio.

Meanwhile, I contacted a man named Bob Benson in Fort

Worth, Texas, and his wife Katty, who had offered to do cabinet work for me. So Barry drove the bus to Fort Worth, and Bob built cabinets for all the television equipment.

In less than six months the Lord took us from one television camera with a twenty-minute portable tape pack, to ownership of more than $100,000 worth of equipment mounted in beautiful cabinets in a completely rebuilt Mercedes-Benz bus.

Our maiden voyage in the bus was to Toledo, Ohio. When we arrived there, a man approached me after our session one night and said, "I was just out looking at your bus, and I noticed that it needs tires. I own a tire store. Would you let me put a new set on for you?"

So along with all the other shiny new things he had provided, God gave us six brand new tires.

That travelling studio has been a gift from the start. When we first bought the bus, it looked like I did when the Lord first got a hold of me. I was a wreck, but through the mercy and the grace of God I have been transformed into a beautiful instrument of his love. So has the bus. It is one of the most attractive buses on the road, and it looks like it was built for television. It really does justice to the sign painted on the back of it: "On the Road for Jesus."

I have no idea where this television ministry is headed, but it has been God's idea from the start. He is directing it, and it will grow as much as he wants it to. If he wants it to remain small, it will remain small. Our only desire is to preach the gospel.

We're not making specific plans, but neither are we planning to stop. We are following the Lord one step at a time. When an opportunity arises, we seize it and move with it. If God's blessing is upon it, it accomplishes his purposes. That's the only way to live the Christian life. You do your best to move when the Lord says move and stop when he says stop. It doesn't matter if your ministry is praying for people in the privacy of your living room or conducting an expensive television program like "Catholic Good News." When the Lord says "go," you've got to go.

When I was first learning how to live like a Christian, Father Jim Smith told me never to compromise the word of God. "Live the word and preach the word," he said. "Don't try to please people. Preach the truth, and let the Holy Spirit convict your listeners."

How right he was! I've learned that it is the Holy Spirit who convicts us of our sinfulness and brings us into a state of holiness. So I preach the word and let the Spirit do his work. But it hasn't always been easy. When I first began to preach, I experienced a great deal of rejection, and I didn't like it. Through Archbishop Patrick Flores of San Antonio, Texas, God freed me from caring what people think of me.

I had spent six months in the San Antonio diocese, preaching to the Catholic prayer groups there. In all that time, I had not met the archbishop. Then one day I was told that he wanted to see me in his office. By the time I arrived I was very nervous. I had never been called in by a bishop before.

When I walked into his office, he looked up from his work and said, "You're Charlie Osburn."

"Yes, Bishop," I replied.

"I've heard many good things about you," he said.

At that statement I breathed a tremendous but silent sigh of relief. However, in the same breath the archbishop said, "I've also heard some bad things. Please sit down."

In an instant my relief changed to terror. I had no idea what he was going to say. I knew that people were getting excited about the church because of my preaching. I knew that people were experiencing physical healing and that marriages were also being healed. But I had no idea how a bishop would receive all this.

"You know, Charlie," Archbishop Flores continued, "I was raised on a farm down in southern Texas near the Mexican border. My father talked to me about Jesus from the time I was a small boy. One of the things he said stuck with me, and it applies to you. My father said, 'You can always identify a man of God by the reports that come after him. There will always be two reports—a good report and a bad report. There will be people healed, and there will be skeptics. Some people will encounter him and come away spiritually blessed. Others will condemn him.' I've heard two reports about you, Charlie. Welcome to my diocese. Is there anything I can do for you?"

That meeting was a great turning point in my life. From that moment on I knew I need not be concerned with what people think of me. If I preach the word in total submission to the bishop that God has placed over me, and if I live what I preach, the Lord will do everything else. There will always be a good report and a bad report, but God doesn't want me to be concerned about it. This discovery liberated me and has enabled me to move forward with my ministry, leaving the worry to God and the authority to those he has placed over me.

My meeting with Archbishop Flores was a forerunner to my contact much later with my own bishop, Rene Gracida. Bishop Gracida had been observing my ministry and wanted to formally give me his blessing, so he wrote me a letter stating his approval of Good News Ministries.

I insist that our schools of evangelization be conducted under the authority of the local Catholic bishop. I refuse to speak in any diocese where the bishop won't give his approval. This frees me, and the parish sponsoring me, from concern about criticism. I've spoken in more than one hundred dioceses in the last six years, and I've yet to be turned down by a bishop.

Neither am I concerned about criticism of my television and radio ministries. I am submitted to my bishop. If he criticizes me, I'll listen. Otherwise, I'll just keep preaching the message God has given me to preach.

At this time our television program continues to grow in

popularity on Trinity. Our radio show is now being aired in many parts of the United States, Canada, and the Philippines, and is picked up by more stations all the time.

The story of the Osburn family's walk in faith continues every day. God keeps opening new doors, and we keep walking through them. Although the radio and television ministry is exciting, my first love and my first priority remains preaching in parishes. Nothing can compare with those week-long seminars where I can stand in the house of Catholic worship, right in the center aisle of the parish church, and preach to Catholic men and women about the role God has appointed for them in life.

Because I so greatly love to preach, I want to devote the last chapter of this book to sharing some reflections on the Nicene Creed, the prayer that we as Catholics recite from memory every Sunday morning in Mass. While it is as familiar to us as the backs of our hands, many of us don't realize how deeply it should influence our daily lives.

NINE

Our Mission for God

THE PROFESSION OF FAITH—the beautiful prayer that Catholics recite every Sunday at Mass—reveals much about the role of lay people in the world. This ancient prayer is a statement not only of what we believe about God and the church, but also of our mission in the church.

Many lay people don't understand that they have a role to play, a mission to accomplish for God. They know the Pope has a mission; they know that the bishops and priests have a mission. But they need to realize that every man, woman, and child also has a mission, by virtue of their baptism, in building God's kingdom through the church.

Considering the Creed line by line can clarify for us our mission as Catholic men and women. It also strengthens our faith in the living God.

The Creed begins, "We believe in one God, the Father the Almighty." There is, in this vast universe, only one God, and he is the Father. He is almighty God, and he created all of mankind—all belong to him, and all are loved by him. By professing this, we acknowledge that there can be no room in our hearts for any kind of prejudice. God is the creator of all, even our enemies. God is the creator of the communists; he is the creator of those whose skin color differs from our own; he is the creator of the primitive Indians in the jungles of South America.

We tend to be prejudiced against people we don't understand, who support what we oppose, or who live in ways we believe are wrong. But in light of the fatherhood of God, we have no choice but to love every human being because God does. If we truly believe what we say when we pray the Creed, if we truly desire to live the way our Father in heaven wants us to live, we must let go of any kind of prejudice.

Each individual is unique, one of a kind, an original creation from the hand of a loving Father. If we believe that we are created by one God, we will see Christian morality in a new light. How can we fight with a brother or a sister, a creature of our heavenly Father? How can we steal from or lie to or gossip about another? How could we want to do anything but love one another by strengthening and serving one another?

If we consider our individuality as sons and daughters of God, we will also realize that God has a unique set of tasks for each of us to perform in his kingdom. No one else can do the things that God has assigned to me to do. He can certainly raise up anyone he wants to, to go to Catholic churches and speak about evangelism. God has given me that job, and he can also give the same kind of work to others. Nevertheless, no one else can do my work. They may be able to stand in the same spot, and teach from the same scriptures, and say the same thing, but no one can do Charlie Osburn's work but Charlie Osburn.

The same is true for every Christian. The Father has special work—a special place in the church—for each of us, and no one else can do that work. No one. If we don't do it, it won't get done. This is sobering but true. And every time we say the Creed, we profess this truth.

The first line of the Creed also tells us that God is the Almighty. He has power and might. He can and will do the things he has promised.

The Creed continues: "creator of heaven and earth; of all that is seen and unseen."

When we recite the Creed, we say that we believe in things we can see ***and*** in things we cannot see. This sounds outlandish! What an amazingly strong faith it must require to say we believe in things we cannot see! Yet we profess this every Sunday.

Before I gave my life to Jesus Christ I would say, "Show me and then I'll believe." But after I gave my life to the Lord, he said to me, "Believe and then I'll show you." That's the difference. The world wants to see and touch and feel before believing (and even then it sometimes rejects the truth). But God says, "Believe in the outlandish things of the Christian faith, and I'll show you that they really do exist." And how much happier we'll be because of that knowledge!

No Christian alive today has ever seen heaven, but we believe that we're going there. God tells us to believe in heaven, and we respond with faith. We believe what God has said, even though we haven't seen it. And when we get to heaven, we will no longer need faith. God will show heaven to us. We won't need to believe in it, because we'll be experiencing it. Faith produces for us the reality of the things we have believed in.

Unfortunately, many Christians have adopted the world's attitude and only believe in what they can see. What a great mistake! We are a people of faith, chosen by God, a holy nation, a people whom God has called to do his work. But this all comes about only because we believe. We can see none of it until we believe in it. Then God makes it real in our life. Our belief places us in a position where we can receive God's gift.

By saying we believe in things unseen, we acknowledge that we believe in love. We can't see love but we know it's real. The same is true of hope and trust and courage. We can't see them, but we know they are real.

This part of our profession of faith can be a great source of hope for those Christians who desire church renewal but are not seeing it in their local church. They should look not so much at what they see in their church, but at the unseen. They should envision the church as full of excited, enthused people on fire with the love and power of the Holy Spirit, doing the work God has called them to do. That's the way I look at the church—in the unseen. I haven't seen complete renewal yet, but I believe in it because it's God's plan for the church; he will bring it to pass.

Notice in these first four lines of the Creed that everything we profess has already been accomplished. God has left nothing undone. He has put everything into position, and he reveals to us the knowledge of things he set in motion long ago. Our response in faith as Catholic Christians is to walk in what God has already done. We don't need to add anything to it; we need only explore what he has done and walk in faith within it.God wants us to walk in faith, believing in him and viewing each other as unique beings created in God's image. God desires that we love what he has done.

Next we profess our faith in God's Son: "We believe in one Lord, Jesus Christ."

The word "lord" means "master." "Landlord" is a similar kind of word. The Lord is the Master, the Owner. When we recite the Creed, we say that we believe that Jesus is our Lord and Master, that he is in charge of our life in the same way a landlord is in charge of a rented apartment. And we are responsible to act accordingly. We need to imitate the Lord Jesus Christ, to live his life, to be like him.

In my travels I have seen many people imitate rock stars. It seems to me that more people imitate rock stars than Jesus. This is tragic. We are the church, and God depends on us to spread the good news of his salvation far and wide. We can only do it if we imitate Jesus Christ.

Why is it so difficult for us to imitate Jesus? We say that we believe that he is the Lord, the Master, the Savior. We say that we believe that he is "the only Son of God, eternally begotten of the Father, God from God, light from light, true God from true God, begotten not made, one in being with the Father; through him all things were made."

We believe that Jesus is "eternally begotten," and that wherever God is, Jesus is. We believe that Jesus has always existed and that all truth, all holiness, all power in the universe reside in him. We believe that Jesus is the only way to the Father. He is the only mediator between God and humans. So why don't we imitate his life? Why don't we give up everything we have in order to be like him, to be with him, to do what he does, to tell everyone we know about him? It makes no sense for us to be lazy about praying or to be sheepish about evangelizing.

If we really do believe these things about Jesus Christ, then we should desire to know him more, to love him more. We should be preoccupied with trying to serve him better and better. We should be consumed with the desire to imitate him. How? By spending time with God in prayer, by spreading the good news of Jesus Christ's love and mercy to everybody we know. God has placed each of us in the world in order to change the world. We are to bring the world into the light of Jesus by evangelizing and doing good works. We have the highest calling there is, and we should remember this every time we say the Creed.

"For us men and for our salvation he came down from heaven. By the power of the Holy Spirit he was born of the Virgin Mary and became man." God in Jesus Christ became a human being, just like you and me. But there are some obvious differences. He was conceived, not by a human father, but by the eternal Father by the power of the Holy Spirit. And he was conceived into the womb of a virgin. God himself, in the form of his eternally begotten Son and by the power of the Holy Spirit, became one of us.

Why? "For us men and for our salvation." God wanted to save us from the mess we had gotten ourselves into. We had been following the world's way. We had been killing and lying and cheating and stealing. God wanted to change all this, so he came into the world as one of us. He taught us how to live. When God tells us to imitate him, he gives us a model, the man Jesus Christ. We can imitate Jesus Christ. We can love like he did. We can share the good news like he did. We can forgive those who trespass against us like he did. Jesus became a human being to show us how to imitate God.

But Jesus was also fully God and was able, by his birth and teaching and death and resurrection, to save us for all eternity. "For our sake he was crucified under Pontius Pilate. He suffered, died, and was buried."

"He suffered, died, and was buried"—for our sake, yours and mine. God loved old Charlie Osburn—an adulterer, a thief, a conniver, a manipulator—so much that he sent his Son to suffer and die. Had I been the only person alive, Jesus would have died for me. Had you been the only person alive, Jesus would have died for you. He suffered and died so that we could be saved and be adopted by God as his own children.

Consider how incredible these truths really are! God created all things for each of us. He sent Jesus into the world for each of us. Everything that God has done he did for each of us as individuals. Simply amazing! Our hearts should be filled with gratitude and the desire to obey God in all things.

Every time that lash struck Jesus' back during his scourging, he accepted it to atone for my sins. Every pain he suffered on the road to Calvary, he suffered for me. Every drop of blood he shed, he shed for me. If God came to earth and did all of that for me, shouldn't I offer what is left of my life to him for his glory? Shouldn't I do everything I can to witness for him? How can I be ashamed of Jesus? He wasn't ashamed of me. He left his privileged place in heaven, took the form of a servant, emptied himself of reputation and possessions, suffered, and died. All for me! I no longer care what the world thinks of me. I care only what Jesus thinks of me. He is the only one I have to be concerned about pleasing. The only reason I am alive is to obey God and witness to Jesus. This is my purpose in life.

This also affects how we look at other people. If God did all these things for every human alive, if he died a redeeming death so that every man and woman might be saved, how can I possibly mistreat anyone? How can I possibly hate or cheat or kill anyone? Jesus lived and died for all. My response must be to love all, to evangelize all, to appreciate all, to refrain from anger with all. That is my responsibility as a Christian.

"On the third day he rose again in fulfillment of the scriptures." For whom did he rise? For me! He came to life on the third day that *I* might have new life in him, that my life might have meaning and purpose. Jesus gave his life that I might be like him and inherit eternal life. And his resurrection proves the truth of all God says. It proves that Jesus really is who he claims to be and that our faith in him is not in vain. He came to life after having died! His body was in the tomb for three days when suddenly, by the power of God, new life came into it, and he rose. The burial wrappings dropped to the ground, and Jesus came out and revealed himself to his apostles. What further proof do we need that everything that we say we believe in is true? None. The resurrection of Jesus proves it all.

"He ascended into heaven and is seated at the right hand of the Father. He will come in glory to judge the living and the dead and his kingdom will have no end."

When Jesus had accomplished all he came to do, he returned to heaven to reign in glory until the day appointed by God for the judgment of all mankind. God's work on earth has been finished by Jesus Christ. Now he wants us to take up the cause and be counted for Jesus. Our life is temporary. The greatest thing we can do during it is to win the world for Jesus. And we do this by evangelizing the people we know one at a time. That is our mission.

When will Jesus come again? I hope he comes today. And

God expects me to evangelize as if Jesus is going to come today, as though everyone I know who has not given his or her life to Jesus will be lost. We need that kind of fervor in proclaiming Jesus Christ.

So far we have analyzed two ministries—those of the Father and of the Son. Both are full and complete. The Father has finished all of his work, and Jesus has finished all of his except for his return at the end of time to close the books of human history, bringing the fullness of God's kingdom—the everlasting kingdom—to the living and the dead.

The rest of the Creed is devoted to the Holy Spirit and to the church, which still have things to do.

"We believe in the Holy Spirit, the Lord and giver of life, who proceeds from the Father and the Son. With the Father and the Son he is worshipped and glorified. He has spoken through the prophets."

By virtue of our baptism and confirmation we have received the Spirit of God. What does the Spirit do for us? The Creed says that the Holy Spirit is "the Lord and giver of life." That means that we who are filled with the Holy Spirit are carriers of life. We not only have life within us, but we bring it to others. We can give life away because that is the nature of the Holy Spirit. He gives away the life of Jesus Christ, and, since he lives in us, he gives away the life of Jesus to others through us.

The Holy Spirit makes us carriers of enthusiasm, of excitement, of joy, of forgiveness, of reconciliation. Each of these is a quality of the everlasting life the Holy Spirit brings to us.

We sometimes look for life in worldly things. We'd rather have a hundred dollars in our pocket than the everlasting life of the Holy Spirit. But money doesn't bring life. Neither does anything or anyone else. Only the Holy Spirit brings life. The Spirit is the life of God, the love of God, the power of God, the wisdom of God. And God puts that same Spirit into our lives so that we can carry life on his behalf.

After I experienced the healing of Jesus Christ and the power of his Holy Spirit, I discovered that I was a carrier of life. I began to use my natural talents to bring people into the kingdom of God. I used the life of the Spirit within me to bring people into an experiential knowledge of Jesus Christ.

What would happen to the world today if the 700 million Roman Catholics did the same? Pope Paul VI said we'd save the world in twenty-four hours. The world is in tragic shape, largely because of our ignorance of the power of God's Holy Spirit.

The Holy Spirit "has spoken through the prophets." We believe that. But do we believe that he continues to speak through the prophets today? Do we believe that the Holy Spirit tells us what God wants us to do as he speaks through prophets like the pope and the fathers of the Second Vatican Council? Every time we recite the Creed, we should remember that he still speaks through the prophets today.

The next part of the Creed brings our faith home to us and makes us aware of our place in God's work in the world: "We believe in one, holy, catholic, and apostolic church."

We know who the church is—the people of God who are baptized and confirmed and who assemble regularly to worship God and hear his word. We know that the church building is not the church; we know that the Vatican and the other institutions are not the church. The individual people—laity, priests, bishops, and pope—together are the church.

What makes the church one, holy, catholic, and apostolic? We are one because the church has one head, Jesus Christ. The pope isn't in charge of the church. Jesus is. The pope is his vicar; he runs some of the machinery of the church on Jesus' behalf. But Jesus is in charge. It is he who makes the church one.

Jesus also makes the church holy. Holiness means that we have God's life within us as a community called the church. God's life in the church—in the sacraments, in the liturgy, and in the various activities and institutions—makes us holy.

Holiness also means being set apart. Jesus has set apart his church—all of us together as Catholics—to bring his life to all people. We are set apart from the world for evangelization and good works. And when we do these things, we are acting out of the holiness Jesus Christ has given to us.

The church is catholic because it is universal. God has blessed it and it has spread all over the world.

That the church is apostolic means that it dates from the time of the apostles. The faith we have received has been handed on in an unbroken chain from the apostles, who received it from Jesus himself. Our bishops are successors of the apostles, and perform the same function for Christ today that Peter and John and the others performed in the early church.

But apostolic means more than a nice neat line of faith handed down through the centuries. For us, being apostolic means acting on our faith as the apostles did. It means proclaiming Jesus Christ as Lord; it means speaking in tongues and performing miracles; it means loving one another with the intense love of those who knew Jesus in the flesh. We can perform an apostolic role today and win the world for Jesus.

The Bible, in the Epistle of James, says that "faith without works is dead." If we keep our faith all to ourselves, it will not bring life to the people who need life. If our faith does not prompt us to be apostolic—to go out and work for Jesus Christ like the apostles did—it is dead. James challenges us, "If you say you have faith, then show me your works." The Lord says to us today: "If you say you love one another, let me see healing, because there is no greater love than the healing that comes from forgiveness, reconciliation, and prayer."

If we really believe that we are the church, and that the church is apostolic, then we—you and I—ought to do the same things that the apostles did. If you don't know what they did, read the first few chapters of the Acts of the Apostles in the Bible. Then ask God to show you how to do those things in your family, in your parish, and in your workplace.

"We believe in one baptism for the forgiveness of sins." When we were baptized into Jesus Christ our sins were forgiven. He freed us from the hold sin had on our lives. We no longer need to walk with sin-consciousness. We can walk in holiness. This is not a boast. It is what baptism does. It doesn't mean we will never sin again. It means that when we do we can repent and receive forgiveness from God. It also means that God will give us all the grace necessary to overcome sin in our lives. Baptism is a wonderful gift from God! Jesus does the work. Our part is to believe it and walk in it.

The Creed ends with these words: "We look forward to the resurrection of the dead and the life of the world to come." We look forward in hope to the completion of God's work at the end of time. We know it hasn't happened yet. The dead have not been raised. The eternal kingdom has not yet come in its fullness. But it is coming. We have God's word on it and we place all our hope in it. We want to work as hard as we can to bring as many people as possible into God's kingdom with us.

The Creed summarizes our faith. It is not the totality of our faith—there is more to our faith than these few words. But the Creed is the basis of our faith. It is the beginning of our small, mustard-seed faith. These words are truth and life and security, and we should teach them to our children.

Catholic adults should know these words well so that they won't need to struggle for their identity. We are a people who believe the truths of the Creed. Through our baptism and confirmation we are royal priests of Jesus Christ, a holy people, a nation set apart to do God's work. We are filled with his Spirit who enables us to believe these truths and to act upon them.

If we really mean the words we say when we recite the Creed, if we really believe in the almighty Father, in Jesus

Christ his Son, in the virgin birth, and all the other profound truths professed in it, we will become obsessed with loving our families, our relatives, our friends, our fellow parishioners, our co-workers, and everyone else we know into the kingdom of God.

Charlie, I want to "give it all to Jesus."

1. Admit that you are a sinner.

   Romans 3:23 "For all have sinned and fall short of the glory of God."

2. Be willing to turn from sin.

   Acts 17:30 "In the past God overlooked such ignorance, but now he commands all people everywhere to repent."

3. Believe that Jesus Christ died for you, was buried, and rose from the dead.

   Romans 10:9–10 "That if you confess with your mouth, 'Jesus is Lord,' and believe in your heart that God raised him from the dead, you will be saved. For it is with your heart that you believe and are justified, and it is with your mouth that you confess and are saved."

4. Through prayer, invite Jesus into your life.

   Romans 10:13 "Everyone who calls on the name of the Lord shall be saved."

   Dear God,
   I recognize that I am a sinner and need your forgiveness. I believe that you sent your son Jesus Christ to die for my sin so that I might have eternal life. I now dedicate my life to Jesus Christ and invite him to be my personal Lord and Savior. Give me strength to live as you command.

   My Decision:

   On ____________________ I, ________________________
   DATE YOUR NAME

   accepted Jesus Christ as my personal Lord and Savior.

5. Grow in your Christian faith.

   1. Read the Bible.
   2. Communicate with the Lord through prayer.
   3. Worship the Lord in a Bible-teaching church.
   4. Fellowship with other believers.
   5. Tell others what Jesus Christ means to you.